T H E
ONE-LIFE
SOLUTION
WORKBOOK

Also by Dr. Henry Cloud

The One-Life Solution

Integrity

Boundaries

9 Things You Simply Must Do

THE
ONE-LIFE
SOLUTION

WORKBOOK

Dr. Henry Cloud

ZONDERVAN

ZONDERVAN.com/
AUTHORTRACKER
follow your favorite authors

ZONDERVAN

The One-Life Solution Workbook
Copyright © 2009 by Dr. Henry Cloud

Requests for information should be addressed to:

Zondervan, *Grand Rapids, Michigan 49530*

ISBN 978-0-310-29367-5

Interior design by Beth Shagene

Printed in the United States of America

09 10 11 12 13 14 15 • 24 23 22 21 20 19 18 17 16 15 14 13 12 11 10 9 8 7 6 5 4 3 2 1

*This book is dedicated to everyone
who desires to find the life
that God has designed for you to have,
and for the courage to live it.
God bless you.*

Contents

Acknowledgments

No books, or workbooks, come together on their own. So, I would like to thank a few people for helping this one find its way:

To Sandy Vander Zicht, my editor at Zondervan, for having the vision to see how a workbook for *The One-Life Solution* could be more than a collection of study questions, but instead a stand-alone tool to help people reclaim their lives.

To Greg Clouse, who did much of the heavy lifting of editorial. You did a great job.

To Jan Miller and Shannon Miser-Marven, my literary agents, who have helped make this kind of project possible. They understood that content bridges between even business and churches, and that God is interested in both.

Getting the Most
from This Workbook

Welcome to *The One-Life Solution Workbook*, based chapter by chapter on my book of the same name. You may have read all or portions of the book, or may be discovering this workbook on its own. Either way, you are about to begin a very exciting and fruitful journey of discovery.

I wrote *The One-Life Solution* because everyone, even very high performers, can find themselves at times losing control of the two most vital resources they have to accomplish the things that are important to them: their time and energy. As a result, the visions they have for their lives, or even for a particular year, month, or day, can elude them.

This workbook experience will help you discover for the first time, or get back in touch with, the vision for your life, and the things that are truly important to you. But you will also discover reasons why your vision has eluded you, and how to finally bring it to fruition. By working through the questions, you also will learn to overcome the obstacles—those repetitive patterns of behavior—that rob you of performance and fulfillment and have gotten in the way of your living the life that God has designed for you. You may even be surprised at how a workbook on reclaiming vision, achieving goals, and recapturing your time and energy (in partnership with God and other people) is at its core a spiritual exercise, and that will be part of the fun.

The workbook can be enjoyed by both individuals and groups. Because the topic of boundaries in the workplace is one most of us deal with on a regular basis, it's a natural for discussing in a small group environment among like-minded friends or colleagues who are interested in finding balance in their lives. Just read a chapter ahead of time, then come together to "compare notes." Also, because the workbook deals with much about our personal lives as well, it lends itself to great small group discussions in circles of friends, or churches. I have seen this material used successfully both among friends and in some of the largest corporations in the world. So find the right context for you and go for it.

As you take this journey, you may find yourself becoming more aware of your own needs and the needs of others. My prayer is that your workplace situation will improve, and your personal life will be more fulfilling as a result of taking a little time, either by yourself or with others, to discover the "One-Life Solution" that God has for you.

God bless,
Henry Cloud, PhD
Los Angeles, California, 2009

Part One

FOUNDATIONS

one

Identifying the Problem — and the Solution

This book is primarily about work, but it is also about you and your well-being as a person. It is about developing a strong, integrated core from which you can live the one life that only you can live.

Sometimes, as the old saying goes, we can't see the forest for the trees. We get so caught up in the problem right in front of us that we can't see what may be causing it—the bigger issue that holds the real solution. Even situations that seem to have very little in common might have the same underlying cause, if only we could see it. Consider the following situations, for example:

- Maria is a CEO who needs to fire a member of her team, but she just can't seem to pull the trigger.
- David is a manager whose bullying boss affects his entire life.
- Ryan is an MBA whose time is always filled and who feels like he never has time for the things that really matter, in both work and his personal life.
- Sophie is a talented creative director who is too unfocused to deliver the results she is capable of delivering.
- Sarah is an executive assistant who feels trapped by her boss's inappropriate behavior, yet she cannot bring herself to speak up or escape the situation.
- Kevin is a salesperson who is stuck at a plateau and cannot break through to the next level of sales.

It would be easy, and make total sense, to jump right in and find a solution to each of these problems: get it over with and fire him, call HR, ignore your boss's comments, take a time management seminar, clarify your priorities, take assertiveness training, or make more cold calls. You can just hear those pieces of advice being offered by trusted friends. But while the advice makes sense, it also misses the point.

All of these problems seem very different on the surface, but in reality, each of these individuals has a common personal issue: *they each have lost control of themselves.* Pressures from other people, the amount of work they have to do, and their own performance challenges leave them unable to do what they truly need or want to do. If that core issue of personal control is not addressed by each person, they will just find themselves in the same or similar situations again. But if they resolve the real cause, they will find freedom in not only their present circumstances but in many other areas of life as well.

Notice the way that each person described above has lost control of themselves:

- Maria is controlled by how the employee is going to feel or react.
- David's emotional life is controlled by his boss's insensitivity.
- Ryan's purpose is thwarted by a lack of control of his time.
- Sophie's goals are out of her reach because she has lost control of her ability to stay on task.
- Sarah is controlled and in prison to a lecherous boss.
- Kevin cannot break past a plateau because he has lost control of some of his talents and abilities.

These people all feel stuck by circumstances and forces out of their control. They have lost control of themselves. But if they could look beyond their present situations, they would also see that this is not the first time they have felt that way. They have experienced feeling controlled, or stuck, before.

1. With which of the six people above do you most closely identify? Why?

2. Name a situation where you knew what you wanted or needed to do but, for some reason—perhaps pressures from the outside or the inside—were not able to do it.

Chances are, you can name several such situations. Make a list of them so that you can see how much the loss of control has affected your life.

THE ONE SOLUTION

If the one underlying issue in these scenarios and in our personal lives is losing control of ourselves, then what is the solution? The one solution, the one answer, is called "boundaries." In each one of the scenarios, the common issue is that no matter what their positions — from CEO all the way to assistant — these people all lacked an internal core or "boundaries" from which they were able to define themselves and express that "defined self" in a way that made life work. The issue of boundaries is one of the biggest issues that each of us will face in business and in life.

Essentially, boundaries keep us from being controlled by forces outside of ourselves. Boundaries are a large part of our ability to have what the Bible calls "self-control," a fruit of the Spirit. A person who has good boundaries is in control of him- or herself and is not controlled by forces on the outside. Boundaries affect the ways we experience work and life, the ways we relate to others in work and life, and the degree to which we are successful in our pursuits. When we lack good boundaries, we suffer in three significant ways:

- In our emotions
- In our relationships
- In our performance

3. With which *emotional* effects of feeling out of control or "stuck" can you identify? (i.e., anxiety, loss of passion, burnout or loss of energy, depression, loss of health, feeling bad or inferior, resentment)

4. With which *relational* effects can you identify? (i.e., your boss or co-worker is difficult; your work is affecting significant relationships in your life at home or otherwise; a co-worker is not doing their job and it is affecting you; you are overwhelmed by someone; you're getting hurt at work; you are afraid to confront someone; a relationship is so bad that you are thinking of leaving a good job to get away)

5. With which *effects on performance* can you identify? (i.e., your workload is getting more and more out of control; you cannot stay focused on the real mission; you feel chaotic, procrastinate or are disorganized; you can't close the deal, have trouble delegating, etc.)

6. In light of how you have responded above, rank on a scale of 1 – 10 how you are doing emotionally, relationally, and in your performance.

- Emotional rank   _____
- Relational rank   _____
- Performance rank   _____

YOU ARE DESIGNED TO HAVE A STRUCTURED CHARACTER

Just as children are designed to begin walking at a certain age, developmental research shows us that we were designed to have a structured, defined character that is free, motivated, powerful, autonomous, aggressive, and initiating. But sometimes we face obstacles that keep us from getting there. When that happens, it is not unusual to become discouraged and think that we cannot change.

The good news is, God designed us to have a structured character and good boundaries. "We are," as Ephesians 2:10 says, "God's workmanship, created in Christ Jesus to do good works, which God prepared in advance for us to do." Not only that, God has promised to help you get there: "being confident of this, that he who began a good work in you will carry it on to completion until the day of Christ Jesus" (Philippians 1:6).

But, all of this points to making a shift in our thinking from just solving "problems" to growing as a person and resolving the real issues that cause our problems. The real need is for our own personal growth. We must get to the things that are eroding our personal power, motivation, drive, autonomy, freedom, good aggression, and initiative. If *we* change, then the problems will get better.

7. What is your level of hope that you can change in these areas?

8. What are your thoughts on God's view of and support of your efforts to regain control of your life, work, and relationships?

Jesus pointed out that if we are healthy as people, we will escape a lot of these kinds of problems. Even in the midst of difficulties, we will prevail if we are mature. But, if we avoid our personal growth, we will be unable to produce the fruitfulness we desire: "No good tree bears bad fruit, nor does a bad tree bear good fruit" (Luke 6:43). In other words, the healthier we (the tree) are, the better our results. And to the extent we are not facing our issues, good fruit will evade us.

9. Where have you seen an organization, a person, or yourself address a problem with someone, only to find that they did not deal with the real issue (i.e., that the person needed to grow in some way)? What was the result?

The call of the One-Life Solution is for us to grow as people and regain what the Bible refers to as "self-control." If we do that, through growing in our boundaries, we will see results in the following areas:

- Our personal power
- Our drive
- Our good aggressiveness
- Our motivation
- Our autonomy and freedom
- Our healthy initiative

10. In which of these areas would you like to improve?

THE CHALLENGE OF REGAINING CONTROL
IN A "STRUCTURELESS" CULTURE

If you are feeling overwhelmed and out of control, there is a good reason! Life today has become so fragmented that it is increasingly difficult to "bring it all together." Life used to be structured by the simple reality that we used to go "to" work and be "at" work for a certain time. When we were not "at work," we were not working: we were "off." There was an implicit balance in the way that we worked and had a personal life.

But, with the Internet, e-mail, PDAs, and cell phones, work can find us anywhere, anytime. We can go home and do e-mail instead of connecting with those close to us. We can answer e-mail on our PDA while attending a child's sporting event. We can be on a date night and be interrupted by an e-mail or call on our cell phone. Work has spilled over into life big-time. If we do not have the internal boundaries to protect us from this, technology will overtake us. All it takes is a boss who hits "send."

11. In which ways has technology increased your workload?

12. In what ways does your cell phone, PDA, or e-mail intrude into your personal life?

What problems does that cause you?

What makes it difficult for you to keep this from happening?

To what extent might your personal loss of control or lack of boundaries be contributing to the problem?

If you see how your time and your energy may have been lost to outside forces, leaving you fragmented and unable to focus on the things that matter the most to you, consider this verse: "See then that ye walk circumspectly, not as fools, but as wise, redeeming the time, because the days are evil" (Ephesians 5:15 – 16 KJV).

13. The word "redeem" can mean "rescued from loss." To what extent can you identify with needing to have your time "rescued?"

14. How much do you truly believe that God cares about your time as much as you do and wants to help you get it back?

15. How do you feel about the prospect that growing in your boundaries can help you not only perform better, but recapture your time and energy, and have a better life?

As you move forward in this workbook, begin with the realization that God did not design you to be overstressed and overwhelmed, out-of-control and fragmented. He designed you for a life of fruitfulness in your emotions, relationships, and your work. As Jesus said, his yoke is easy and his burden is light. Often, we do not realize that it is our own issues that are making it so difficult. The goal of this study is personal spiritual growth that affects your performance and well-being. With that hope, we move on, to realizing exactly what that vision can be.

PRAYER

God, thank you that you have given life to me and that you have a plan for me. I accept the fact that no matter what circumstances I face, resolving them is going to involve my getting better in some way. Help me to see where I need to grow so that I might fulfill your plan for me and also be fulfilled in these key areas of life. Give me the wisdom, power, and help that I need to make all of this come to fruition. Help me to find the ultimate use of my time and my energy to fulfill your purposes for me. Amen.

two

Your Vision and Your Boundaries

Most people are so caught up in trying to control what they cannot control that they lose control of themselves.

In the words of Steven Covey, it's important to "begin with the end in mind." So what is the end we are trying to accomplish?

To gain control

The objective is not to gain control of other people, or of all the circumstances, or even all of the outcomes. Those things will take care of themselves as you gain control of the only thing you can ever control—yourself—and begin to experience the life you desire. But in order to gain control, you need a vision of what you are trying to accomplish by building good boundaries.

What if each day, when you get up, you know that you will spend the day:

- Fully engaged, pouring yourself into the things that matter to you
- Doing your work well, getting great results
- Enjoying the process and the relationships that come with it
- Facing problems with a feeling of competence and working through difficulties well
- Getting tired, but not burned out in the process
- Having the satisfaction that you spent the day focusing on the things that matter most to you and that all of your efforts were spent well

1. Which elements of that vision are the most attractive to you?

Do you feel that such a life is possible? Do you know people who seem to live that way?

Certainly that kind of life sounds good, but is it really possible? Before you write it off as impossibly idealistic, think about it. You had better hope it *is* possible — the alternative does not sound good at all. Consider such a scenario:

- You wake up dreading another day in which you will feel disengaged as you pour your time and energy into things that do not matter to you
- You may or may not get results, as it feels so out of your control
- The process and the relationships will bring you down
- You feel de-motivated
- The challenges feel overwhelming and you fear they will get the best of you
- You know you will feel drained and burned out at the end and that rest will do little to help
- When you look back, you will feel that little that you did had much meaning to things that really matter to you

2. With which aspects of this vision do you identify?

What is the result, in your life and in the lives of people you know, when people live this way?

CREATING A VISION

When our boundaries and self-control are diminished, it is easy to lose our sense of well-being and our hope for a prosperous future. Each person described in chapter 1, for example, felt unable to prosper in those situations. But that is not God's vision for us, nor should it be our vision for ourselves.

To have a better understanding of God's vision for us and what it might look like to create a vision for your life, consider what the Bible has to say about your well-being and potential for life. For example, Moses writes: "The LORD commanded us to obey all these decrees and to fear the LORD our God, so that we might always prosper and be kept alive, as is the case today" (Deuteronomy 6:24). The word "prosper" here means a broad sense of well-being, much like the first vision.

3. What does this verse say to you about what is possible?

The psalmist writes, "The LORD be exalted, who delights in the well-being of his servant" (Psalm 35:27).

4. What do you think about the idea that God delights in your well-being?

In what ways does this idea bring hope, and how does it influence your view of God?

Not only does God delight in our well-being, Romans 8:37 reminds us that "in all these things we are more than conquerors through him who loved us."

5. In what ways does this promise give you hope that you are not designed to be a victim of life acting upon you, but that no matter what happens, you have the power to overcome the challenge?

John goes on to say that "everyone born of God overcomes the world. This is the victory that has overcome the world, even our faith" (1 John 5:4).

6. When you look at your life from that perspective, what hope do you have that you do not have to be a victim, but that you can be victorious in life?

Which specific situations in terms of how you feel, your relationships, your performance, and your spirituality would you like to turn into victories?

The message of this book is that you are not a victim of circumstances and problems. Life does not simply act upon you; you act upon life. You are not a *result*, but a *cause*. Your choices and actions bring about the results you want in your work and in your life, as opposed to your work and your life bringing about results on you.

WHAT IS A BOUNDARY?

Pure and simple, a boundary is a property line that defines where you end and where someone or something else begins. In the physical world, property lines are relatively easy to see or to figure out. For example, a property line defines where your yard ends and your neighbor's begins. Often, a physical marker such as a fence or a wall shows where that line is. Your house also has physical walls that define it and give it structure and definition. It is easy to determine precisely where the house is and to know what is inside the house and what is outside.

Boundaries are easy to see and understand in the physical world, but what about in the personal and interpersonal world? How do boundaries provide definition and structure there? Let's take a look at six key areas that will help us understand how personal boundaries work.

Ownership

People with good boundaries feel as if their feelings, thoughts, choices, desires, opinions, behaviors, talents, and whatever else goes on in their lives belong to them.

7. To what extent do you feel that your life and work belong to you?

Do you, for example, fully own what goes on in your heart, mind, and soul? If not, why not?

Do you, for example, fully own your thoughts, passions, and choices? If not, why not?

8. Who do you feel has more ownership of some part of your life than you do? How did you lose ownership to that person?

Control

Owners get to do whatever they want to do with their own property. People with good boundaries realize that they are in control of the things that are theirs alone to control, such as their feelings, choices, behaviors, and attitudes. While they often cannot control the external realities within which they find themselves, they can control their response to those realities.

If they feel bad because they have a bullying boss, for example, they realize that the boss does not control how they feel. Only they control how they feel. They also realize that they cannot control their boss's actions. So they begin to take control of what they can control—themselves. They begin to see that they are not powerless victims, but that they can do what is necessary to feel better, regardless of how their boss behaves.

9. To what extent do you feel that you are in control of the things that are only yours to control, such as what goes on in your heart, mind, and soul?

In what ways do you feel that you are a victim of someone else's dysfunction, bullying, or other behavior that gives them more control of some part of your life than you have?

10. What are your responses to these verses which clearly say that God wants you to have control of yourself?

Galatians 5:22–23	But the fruit of the Spirit is love, joy, peace, patience, kindness, goodness, faithfulness, gentleness and self-control. Against such things there is no law.
2 Peter 1:5	For this very reason, make every effort to add to your faith goodness; and to goodness, knowledge;
2 Peter 1:6	and to knowledge, self-control; and to self-control, perseverance; and to perseverance, godliness;
2 Peter 1:7	and to godliness, brotherly kindness; and to brotherly kindness, love.

2 Peter 1:8   For if you possess these qualities in increasing measure, they will keep you from being ineffective and unproductive in your knowledge of our Lord Jesus Christ.

Freedom

The idea of self-control of your own property gives rise to the concept of freedom. It is totally your choice what to do with your property. You are the one who controls it, and you have the power to do with it what you want.

When it comes to work, a person in control realizes that he or she is not a victim. No one is holding a gun to his or her head, so there is freedom to make whatever choices he or she wants to make. When you begin to make choices based on decisions that you own and for which you take responsibility, a whole world of choices opens up to you. You are totally free to make whatever choices you please.

11. How free do you feel inside?

12. Which of the good options available to you are you exercising?

Which of the real freedoms that you possess are you taking advantage of?

13. In which ways are you limiting your own freedom?

Responsibility, Accountability, and Consequences

Ownership, control, and freedom all come with responsibility, accountability, and consequences. You can do what you want to do, but you also will reap the consequences of what you choose to do, good or bad. When you have boundaries, you know that whatever the consequences of your choices are, those consequences are your responsibility, and you are not at odds with that reality. You take responsibility for where your choices lead you, whether the choice is good or bad, smart or dumb.

14. To what extent do you take responsibility for the consequences of your choices, your attitudes, beliefs, and feelings?

In which areas is this most difficult for you?

15. In which situations or relationships do you take on consequences that others should be taking on for themselves? What is the result?

16. How do you let the consequences of your own choices speak to you and direct you toward action?

17. Which consequences in your life right now do you need to let speak to you and motivate you to change?

Limits

If you own your property and are free to control what goes on there, then you are also free to limit what goes on there. If people trespass or do something on your property, you can have them removed from your property, and you can hold them accountable for the damages they caused. But it is up to you to take control and to set the limits of what you will and will not allow. Limits also apply in saying no to yourself in terms of what you allow yourself to agree to, making sure that you do not agree to do things past your personal limits of time and energy, or against your values.

18. How well do you set limits with others and with yourself?

What aspects of setting limits are hard for you?

19. If there is a person right now with whom you need to set a limit, what is keeping you from doing it?

20. Think of someone you know who is good at setting limits and consider what they do. What can you learn from that person's example, and how does following their example feel to you?

Protection

When you know where your boundaries and limits are, and you are in control of that property, then you can do something very important. You can keep the good things inside your property and the bad things out. Your boundaries protect the things that are valuable to you that you want to stay inside, safe from the forces that might come to steal or destroy them.

Those who are in control of themselves can stand up to persons or circumstances that threaten to hurt them. They have the boundaries to protect themselves, others, and their organization and its mission from forces and people who wish to cause them harm.

21. How secure and clear is your fence that says "keep out" to people and their behaviors that are not good for you?

22. How often do you allow wolves to get into your yard or allow toxic people to dump whatever sludge they wish onto the property of your heart, mind, and soul?

What weakness in your boundaries allows this to happen?

23. Which things of value are you not protecting right now?

What steps can you take to better protect those assets?

Here is the reality. If you do not have good personal and interpersonal boundaries, you begin to find your "yard" collecting the trash that surrounds you or filling up with more tasks to do than you desire. Life gets junky, and pretty soon you don't much like living there. Unfortunately, when the property is you, you can't sell or move. The only answer is to build some fences, take ownership, and reclaim control of your life.

In light of your desire for a clean "yard" where you truly want to live, take the time to focus your thoughts on Psalm 1:1–3 (TNIV):

> Blessed are those
> who do not walk in step with the wicked
> or stand in the way that sinners take
> or sit in the company of mockers,
> but who delight in the law of the LORD
> and meditate on his law day and night.
> They are like a tree planted by streams of water,
> which yields its fruit in season
> and whose leaf does not wither—
> whatever they do prospers.

PRAYER

Dear God, help me to develop a vision for my life and my work that is in line with how you designed life to be. Show me where I have settled for something less. I understand and accept that this does not mean that bad things won't happen to me, but I do ask that you will help me to respond to bad things in a way that I am not victimized and enables me to be victorious. Help me to be a cause and not a result. Help me to see where my boundaries need to improve. Show me what I need to know and need to do, and I will follow you. Amen.

three

Structure and Boundaries

Your boundaries are the structure of your personality, and,
as you live them out, they organize the structure of your self,
your relationships, your work, and your life.

In the physical world, the structures of boundaries are easy to see, like fences and walls. If we ignore those structures, we will feel the consequences—such as when we bump into a wall or scratch ourselves on a barbed wire fence. But in the personal and interpersonal world, the structures of boundaries are not so easy to visualize. They have to be acted out, expressed, and enforced. When they are not clearly identified, confusion, insecurity, and misunderstanding will result.

To better understand how the structures of boundaries work, think of someone who has a well-defined identity and structure to his or her personality.

1. What is it about that person—actions, decisions, words, responses, or interaction with others—that reveals who he or she is?

What do these expressions of that person tell you about him or her?

What is it like to be around that person?

In contrast, think of someone who is more "squishy," someone who you may not be able to clearly define, or whose responses you may not be able to anticipate.

2. What do you feel you really know about that person in terms of:

Where he or she really stands on a particular issue?

What he or she would say to another person?

How he or she would respond in a specific situation?

What he or she really hopes to accomplish?

What is it like for you to be around this person?

3. Which person—well-defined or "squishy"—would you want to be more like?

What about that person appeals to you and why?

In what ways do you think your relationships or interactions with other people might change if you were to become more like that person?

HOW STRUCTURE DEVELOPS

Structure is essential to the development of our character and to our becoming secure, effective, and successful people. As we grow up, we internalize the discipline and structures we experience from others (parents and caretakers), and they become a part of our internal makeup. The interplay of earning rewards and getting into trouble provides the foundational structure for building the kind of self-discipline and self-control that empowers us to fulfill (or hinders us from fulfilling) our life's destiny.

The wisdom of understanding the role of structures and using them well is noted in the ancient proverb: "Train a child in the way he should go, and when he is old he will not turn from it" (Proverbs 22:6). Consider for a moment how this proverb speaks to your own experience:

4. Which kinds of limits or structures were most influential in your development as a person?

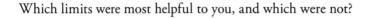

Which limits were most helpful to you, and which were not?

5. Which structures and disciplines do you feel that you lack "inside"?

In what ways does your awareness of the structures you do or do not possess help you to understand and even accept some of your difficulties?

As we mature, we realize that we have the power to make good things happen by making certain choices, and that by not making certain choices we may experience bad things that we do not want. The wisdom of this principle is expressed in the teachings of Scripture:

Remember this: Whoever sows sparingly will also reap sparingly, and whoever sows generously will also reap generously. (2 Corinthians 9:6)

Do not be deceived: God cannot be mocked. People reap what they sow. Those who sow to please their sinful nature, from that nature will reap destruction; those who sow to please the Spirit, from the Spirit will reap eternal life. (Galatians 6:7–8 TNIV)

6. What do these verses say to you in terms of the choices you have made and the results you have experienced?

7. To what extent have you been ignoring the reality of your choices or refusing to exercise your power to choose? What has been the result?

8. In which ways do you see both the positive and the negative sides of the "If I do 'A,' then 'B' will happen" law at work in your life or in the lives of others?

What are some areas in which you want to apply that law to bring about different results in your life?

WHAT STRUCTURE DOES FOR US

Structure helps to build and enforce our integrity through six key functions: differentiation and separateness; containment; definition; limits; values; self-control, freedom, and autonomy.

Differentiation and Separateness

Differentiation is the process whereby children find out who they are as distinct people; the process whereby we begin to own our desires, thoughts, preferences, and uniqueness.

9. Think back to your childhood and identify a memory that indicates you were beginning to differentiate and separate from your parents.

10. Are you aware of areas in which you need to be more separate? Describe them.

    What makes it difficult for you to stand separate and differentiated from the people and situations that pressure you to conform to someone else's idea of who you ought to be?

11. How comfortable do you feel when you express your differences to others, and how do you feel when others express their differences to you?

    What does this reveal to you about the status of your structure and boundaries?

Containment

Containment is to keep something that is destructive or harmful within limits or under control. It prevents the expansion of something bad. It is essential to good leadership.

12. In which situations have you seen a leader exercise containment well? What were the results?

In which situations have you seen a leader manage containment poorly? What were the results?

13. How well do you contain toxic or destructive things *around you* and keep them from spreading?

How well do you contain your *own* toxicity?

What might you do differently to have a better result?

Definition

Definition comes from knowing, owning, and communicating the elements of personhood: your feelings, attitudes, behaviors, choices, limits, thoughts, talents, desires or wants, values, and loves.

14. Which of these elements of personhood do you feel that you have a good, clear definition of and do a good job of knowing and expressing to others?

In what ways do you see these components of definition having a positive impact on your relationships and your effectiveness in your work?

15. Which elements of personhood are more difficult for you to identify and own?

Why do you think that is, and how would you like to grow in that area?

16. What are your "underground fences," the hidden elements of personhood, that you need to make more visible to others?

In what ways is keeping these elements hidden hindering your effectiveness in life and on the job?

Limits

Limits are the essence of your property line as a person. They define how far you are willing to go and where you draw the line. They help compose the structure, shape, and outcome of your life. The key to doing well is to obey your own limits and to respect the limits of others.

17. Which of your personal limits are you good at enforcing, and which ones do you struggle to stay within? Why?

Who are you allowing right now to push you too far or to step over a line that defines your limits?

Which limits of others do you have difficulty respecting?

18. What is your response to the statement "I can safely say that I have never seen a long-term successful person who did not have a good sense of personal limits"?

If you can think of such a person, was the person truly successful in all areas over the long haul, or did a lack of limits catch up with the person in some way?

19. Which limits have you observed as being problematic for people who would otherwise be viewed as successful?

What limits have you noticed or admired in successful people you have known?

Values

To value something is to view it as precious or of high worth. What we value is ultimately what we stand for, what we devote our resources to, and what we are willing to fight for.

20. What are the things you believe you value most? (Go ahead, make the list!)

What is the relationship between what you put on your list and your actions—your expenditures of time, money, and energy?

What do you learn about what you truly value from the disconnects between your list of values and your expenditures?

What does this reveal to you about the structure of your personal identity?

Self-control, Freedom, and Autonomy

Self-control is the ability to exercise control over our feelings, desires, behaviors, and impulses. When all is said and done, good boundaries put us in control of the only person we truly can control: ourselves. Control over oneself is the essence of true power. It involves an internal "No" and "Go" switch that allows a person to exercise self-control by saying "No" to some things and by deciding to "Go" for other things.

21. To what extent can you say yes and no when needed?

To what extent do forces from the inside or outside disable your "No" and "Go" switch and cause you to lose self-control?

22. Do you find it harder to say yes, or harder to say no?

In which situations or with which people, and why?

What price are you paying when you say yes in some situations in which you should be saying no or when you hold back when you should be saying yes?

THE RESULT—IF ALL GOES WELL

If all goes well in our development, we will have strong personal structures that give us the abilities to:

- Experience ourselves as separate and differentiated from others.
- Contain destruction and keep it from spreading.
- Define ourselves and know who we are.
- Set limits when needed.
- Possess and live out values.
- Have self-control and thereby be free and autonomous.

23. As you consider how you experience life, give yourself a numerical (1–5) or grade (A-B-C) rating on *each* of the above. (Just write your rating next to the bullet point.) What does your "grade" in each area say to you about the integrity and strength of your boundaries?

Since we know how structure is developed and how it is broken, we also have hope that we can fix it if it is weak or broken. The psalmist wrote of such hope in Psalm 25:21: "May integrity and uprightness protect me, because my hope is in you."

24. If you think of structure and identity relating to personal integrity, what does this verse say to you about what structure accomplishes for us and where it ultimately comes from?

What is your response to the hope of having structures that provide personal integrity, strength, and self-control when you include God in the picture?

PRAYER

Dear God, I realize that how I was raised and my other past experiences have influenced who I am today. I am painfully aware that I am not the most mature, secure, or effective person that I could be. I accept the reality of my past, both good and bad. I think I missed some things in my structuring experiences that I need now. Please help me in the areas that I have identified to find the experiences, the strength, the will, and the help for those structures to be made stronger in me from this day forward. Amen.

Part Two

REBUILDING
BOUNDARIES

four

Reclaiming Your Power

Decades of research have shown that the degree of powerlessness that people feel directly correlates with diminished functioning.

Deb is a successful businesswoman, but she had one relationship in which she frequently lost personal power because she could not maintain control of her boundaries. Whenever this particular person wanted time from Deb, even when she did not have it to give, she was unable to say "no." As a result, she lost valuable time and energy that she wanted to devote to her family and her work.

Upon deeper reflection, Deb realized that the weakness in her boundaries was her inability to deal with the person's anger or disappointment with her. If she said "no" to one of his requests, he would be upset with her and she could not bear it. So each time he wanted something, she lost control of her agenda.

Deb was experiencing what is referred to as a "power drain." Her power to be in control of herself was lost because of her inability to be okay when this person was upset with her.

1. In what ways do you identify with Deb and her loss of personal power?

Is there a particular person (or more than one) who is able to gain control over you because you fear disappointing him or her?

PERSONAL POWER AND POWER DRAINS

Power is important. You can't live without it, and you are designed to have it in the form of self-control. When you lose self-control, you become controlled by others and are rendered powerless.

The loss of personal power and freedom, which the Bible refers to as slavery or bondage, is the bedrock of losing self-control. It is so important that freedom is referred to as the very reason that Christ died: "It is for freedom that Christ has set us free. Stand firm, then, and do not let yourselves be burdened again by a yoke of slavery" (Galatians 5:1).

2. As you consider this verse, what are your thoughts about how important freedom is to God?

In what ways does this verse encourage you to exercise the power of self-control in your life?

We can lose power in a variety of ways, and we must guard against that loss by discovering our personal weak spots that allow power losses to happen. For example, if Deb did not have the weak spot of fearing someone's disappointment, then she would not lose control.

So, one of the most important questions we can ask ourselves is, "Where are our power drains?"

3. In which relationships or under which circumstances do you tend to lose your ability to control yourself and experience a power drain?

4. In general, how would you describe the chinks in your armor, the holes in your fences?

IDENTIFY THE HOLES IN YOUR FENCES

So, let's get honest, at least with ourselves, and take a hard look at a variety of unhealthy needs, fears, inabilities, and other conditions that tear holes in our boundaries and cause us to lose control. Go through the following list — there are nineteen items in all — and identify the holes in your fences. While all of them may not apply, you can probably identify with some of them. The first two are followed by examples of the kinds of questions you might want to ask yourself as you proceed. The rest provide space to comment on needs and fears that apply to you.

The Need For Security

When the immediate or intermediate future looks uncertain, do you begin to give away something of yourself to maintain security? If the job market looks scary, do you take some assignment that you would not readily agree to if you had the stomach to wait it out, thereby losing control of yourself and your direction? Or, because of fear, do you take on too much work, even with clients you do not want, because you are afraid something may go bad? I am not talking about good diligence here. I am referring to a pattern of operating out of fear.

5. In the face of uncertainty, do you tend to give away too much of yourself just to feel secure? If so, how?

The Need For Approval

Do you have a need for others to like you and always approve of you? When they don't, do all of your systems begin to fire? Do you obsess about it after work and worry about it at work? Are you overly vigilant in wondering what someone's opinion is of you, and if it ever seems to diminish, do you begin to dance and try to fix it until things are good again?

6. Does your need for others to like you and always approve of you cause you to lose power in some way? If so, how?

7. Do you obsess and worry if someone is not pleased with you and lose time and energy over it? When?

The Need to Be Perfect

If the possibility of something not looking good is anywhere on the screen, do you get motivated to action? While striving for excellence is a great trait, perfectionism is not. It gets you dancing around, spending time on things that are not worth spending time on, just because you cannot stand for them to be less than ideal. The need to get it right has turned into the need to have it perfect, and you spend hours and fret and stress over things that others are able to let go.

The Need to Have Others See You As Ideal

This is the motivation to be seen in a certain light and expending lots of energy to manage your image in the eyes of others. I have seen people literally lose a month's energy and focus because they had a small interaction with someone they deemed important that left the impression they were not as good as they desired to be perceived. They were more motivated to work on fixing that impression than they were to address things that were truly important.

The Need to Overidentify with Other
People's Problems, Pain, or Hurt

When other people are in pain, are you not able to stand it? Do you move in to rescue them from it? If you fear that confronting them might cause them pain, do you avoid the needed conversation to spare them the pain of going through it? Does their pain make it difficult for you to discipline them or make decisions that negatively impact them?

The Need to Rescue

This is the tendency to look at someone who is not getting it done and be too much of a helper. Are you the kind of person who cannot stand to see someone get in over his head or have more to do than he seems to be able to manage? So you go into his yard and help him clean it up. Helping others and pitching in is a good quality, but this is different. It is the continuing pattern of getting drawn into doing things for people that they should be doing for themselves.

The Fear of Being Alone or Isolated

Have you never gotten to that step of emotional independence in which being alone, at least for a while, feels good? So sometimes when it would be good for you to be alone, do you lose your direction and the objectives that are important to you just to be around people? You feel you have to go to lunch with that group or to that seminar, even when it would serve you better to stay in the office and complete something or work at home that day. Or, maybe just for the sake of being on a team, you give away too much of yourself. Does a fear of being alone cause you to not be able to take a stand at times?

The Fear of Conflict and Need for Harmony

Do you get really uncomfortable when there is a conflict and people are not feeling harmonious? If there is disruption in the unity or togetherness for a time, is it difficult for you to allow that to be and just sit with it? Do you quickly seek out people to fix things or restore harmony, when often it would be better to let them fret or think about it?

The Fear of Disagreement or Differing Opinions

Do you feel that having different opinions is somehow a negative thing, no matter what side of the equation you are on? When you disagree with someone, do you feel like you have done something bad or hurt their feelings in some way, just by disagreeing with them? Or, when someone disagrees with you, do you take it as meaning something other than just a different opinion, such as an indication that you are wrong or inferior or stupid or some other personal meaning?

The Fear of Anger

Maybe you come from a background in which there was a lot of hurtful anger, or even abuse, and have suffered at the hands of angry people. So are you extra sensitive to it, such that whenever someone is angry or even might become angry you dance to their tune and lose yourself to make sure that they are okay? Or do you avoid conflict with them, avoid saying what you think to keep them from being angry?

The Fear of Feeling Inferior

Perhaps you have never really owned your own strengths, talents, and abilities, and you are still feeling sort of inferior to others. Do you feel a little like a kid and others are all adults? Do you feel that they are smarter, better, or above you in some way? If you do, do you give away your power to whatever they want or think and not speak up when you really do have something to contribute? Do you just fold your cards instead and defer to the "real" experts?

The Fear of Someone's Position or Power

Sometimes we do not just give power to a person in our heads. They actually possess it in reality, like a boss. This person does have power over you in a certain sense, in that they are in control of your job. But, does the way you experience people having power over you exceed the amount of fear and respect that is normal? Does it take on the extra dimension of being able to define you, make you feel little, stupid, or powerless? As a result, do you notice that you are not yourself with someone who is over you?

The Inability to Say No

There is a power dynamic in all relationships. In the good ones, it is mutual. Each person shows up with who they are, their thoughts and opinions, wants, likes and dislikes, and puts it out there for the other person to bump up against. That is a real relationship. But, some cannot stand the force of another person's presence, another person's wants. They just by nature cave in. They blink first. How comfortable are you with standing up to another's request or wishes? Can you say no? Do you fold to other's thoughts, wants, likes, and dislikes just because to not blink is too uncomfortable?

The Inability to Hear No or Accept Limits

Sometimes it is not the tendency to back down that causes you to get out of control. It is the opposite. You fight and protest anytime someone says no to you or you encounter a limit or opposition. Is your problem with boundaries not that you give yours up, but that you encroach on the boundaries of others and are a control freak? Are you described by people as controlling or aggressive? Whenever you run into a boundary of anyone else and cannot be in control, do you protest and try to push them into giving in to you? (If you can't answer this one, ask someone who works with you.)

The Inability to Tolerate the Imperfection, Incompetence, Nonperformance, or Failure of Others

Do you lose yourself, your values, your emotional well-being, and stability when someone else is not doing their job? Are you the type who cannot stand nonperformance, and it makes you crazy? As a result, you lose control of yourself and act in ways that are not helpful, either to the person, or to your own goal of making it all work out well. Irresponsible people make you crazy, and as a result, you lose it and act in ways that do not help. Also, you might miss out on seeing the good parts of some people as well.

Idealization and Hero Worship

We all have people that we see as special or incredible in some way. That is a good thing. For example, if I played golf with Jack Nicklaus, my boyhood hero, I would feel like I were with a godlike figure. But sometimes when people idealize someone, for whatever reason, they cease to be a person around them. They fawn over them and give that person too much power over them, trying to please them or always get on their good side. Do you play up to the person you have put up on the pedestal and give away much of your personhood just because you idealize them? Do you kind of lose your own brain and choices?

Lack of Internal Structure

It may not take a person or a situation to get you out of control. It may just take being awake. Are you impulsive by nature, a perpetual ADD type who just cannot sit within the bounds of any limit? If so, it is costing you. Your impulsivity—your inability to live within the limit of good structure—is taking its toll on you and/or some significant relationships to you, in and out of work. Sometimes people lose their power and effectiveness because they are out of control by nature. They are just impulsive and have never resolved that tendency.

Dependency

Are you dependent on others to help define who you are? Do you lack a sense of personhood and look to others for validation, approval, significance, input, thoughts, security, etc.? Maybe something has happened in your development that has left you lacking that intact feeling of being an independent person in your own right, and as a result you are overly dependent on the judgment and input of others.

Vulnerability to Bad Conditions or Outcomes

Are you fine as long as things are going well, but, under stress, you become someone else? Do you lose yourself or withdraw and get overly stressed? You might get controlling or angry or argumentative. You might get scared and overreact in a myriad of situations, losing your best judgment and abilities. Either way, under stressful conditions, you lose ownership of your best self out of fear and anxiety. Maybe it is a loss of control or a fear of failure, but when things are not good, neither are you.

If you did not identify with at least one of these needs, fears, inabilities, or conditions, then you live in a cave and you need to get out more! All of us face situations and people that get to our underbelly and turn us into less than who we want to be. Becoming aware of your patterns and when you use them is a key step in getting better.

REGAINING POWER OVER POWER DRAINS

God created us to have power, just as he does. While we are not omnipotent as he is, we are designed to have the power of self-control and to live without being controlled by fears. We are not to be intimidated by others, but are to have a fearless and sound mind as Paul describes in 2 Timothy 1:7: "For God hath not given us the spirit of fear; but of power, and of love, and of a sound mind" (KJV).

8. As you consider this verse, what are your thoughts about the concept of "power drains" and God's role in helping you to overcome them?

9. If you are living under a spirit of fear or another kind of power drain, how much do you want to end its control over your life?

There is hope! Finding your power drains is the first step toward ending them. In the next chapter, we will take the next step toward resolving them.

PRAYER

Dear God, I thank you that you designed me for freedom and that you care about helping me to reclaim the power and self-control I have lost. Please help me to find the sources of my power drains. Show me the steps I need to take in order to reclaim control of myself, my work, and my life. Amen.

five

The Audit

The power of the audit is that it reveals where your resources
have been going and empowers you to redirect them where
you really want them to go.

"What happened to all my money?" is a feeling that everyone has had at some time. You may get the monthly profit and loss statement, and gasp, "What? Where did all of that revenue go?" Or, you may look at your personal checkbook and wonder how there wasn't more left over at the end.

What happens next is crucial. Smart people do a category-by-category audit and analysis to regain their power in managing their resources. If the cost of goods is way out of line, they find out why and have a serious talk with suppliers. If G and A is too big a slice of the pie, they find out why and cut the fat. They do whatever it takes to free up resources to spend on the things that matter most—new business investment, infrastructure that fuels growth, more sales people, research and development, better employee pay, or distribution of profit to shareholders. The goal is to maximize resources in order to bring your real purposes to fruition.

The power of the audit is that it reveals where your resources are going, perhaps in ways that you were not aware of and did not want, and empowers you to redirect them to where you really want them to go. Further, it brings insight into why your resources were being drained away. Resources do not just disappear for no reason. There is always a why and a how, good or bad.

1. Have you ever done an audit of how you spend your time? If so, what did you learn? How did you put that information into practice? What difference did it make in your life?

If not, how do you think a time audit could help you in your work and personal life?

2. To what extent do you view your time as being as important a resource as money, and how might your view be affecting your effectiveness in your work and personal life? (If you really think about it, how you spend your time is where your money actually comes from. So, it *is* as important, and actually more important, because it gives us much more than money.)

YOUR TIME IS YOUR LIFE

Just as money is a precious resource to further the purposes of a business and, therefore, must be spent carefully and intentionally, time is a precious resource for life too. Your time *is* your life. Period. How you spend it ends up being what your life is. No matter what you want to do, wish you had done, plan to do, or fantasize about while you are doing something else, the final reality of your life is how you spend your time. Turning your time into the life that you want involves more than time management. It requires you to find out why you are losing control of your time and then taking steps to regain it.

3. What is your reaction to the statement "Your time *is* your life"?

In what ways do you currently think about your time and schedule as being your life?

Even when we try to manage our time, our best-laid plans may not end up happening as we would like. The reason is, other issues get in the way and interrupt our plans. For example:

- The talkative person (the one who never draws a breath) wanders into your office or calls you.
- You leave your desk, or call someone to "ask a quick question," but find that it is you who lingers to talk more than necessary.
- Because you want it to be perfect, you reread an e-mail, report, or letter several times before you send it.
- You often get distracted from important tasks by an e-mail, Web surfing, or some other interruption.
- You find it hard to switch your phone or Blackberry to voice mail or shut down your e-mail while you are working.
- When an e-mail comes in, you feel compelled to answer it right then because you feel the sender is expecting an immediate response.

4. Which of these reasons for losing control of your time could you identify with?

Which other reasons for losing control of time would you add to the list?

How much time do you think you might be losing to reasons such as these, and how much of an obstacle to the life you want might they be?

THE AUDIT

Our time and energy are what actually produce results in our work and life. But we often do not know what we are spending our time on nor why. We may feel overworked, stressed out, spread too thin, and dissatisfied, yet, we have not connected the dots to see that our results are a function of how we spend our time. Just as a financial audit reveals where the money is going, the time audit reveals where our time—the most valuable resource we possess—is going. The audit will reveal three areas of awareness about time that will help to reclaim that powerful resource.

Awareness 1: Know Where You Spend Your Time

This, the first result of the audit, will give you a real, factual, objective picture of where you spend your time, i.e., "where you spend your life." It will reveal what you are truly investing in regardless of what you want to be (or think you are) investing in.

The reality is, we are very subjective about ourselves and our actions. Perhaps that is why Ephesians 5:15–16 reminds us, "Be very careful, then, how you live—not as unwise but as wise, making the most of every opportunity." This is not something we do easily on our own.

5. How "careful" would you say you are in following the advice of this verse to spend your time wisely?

6. Where would you say that the big chunks of time in your life go, and how certain are you of your estimates?

7. How eager are you to find out the real truth about your time? What might be your concerns about finding out the truth, such as the potential for having to make changes or creating conflict with a person you care about?

Awareness 2: Discover the (Dis)connections Between
Your Values and How You Spend Your Time

The audit makes you aware of the relationship between how you spend your time and your stated values, purpose, mission, gifts, and objectives.

8. How closely aligned do you think your time will be to the things you have said are important to you?

9. Have you ever written down clear statements of vision, mission, and key objectives for your different areas of life (personal, professional, spiritual, etc.)? If so, how would you compare your current reality to what your vision, mission, and objectives say?

Awareness 3: Identify the Personal Issues
That Contribute to the Problem

Time does not simply "slip away," we usually "give it away." There is a reason we make the choices we make, a reason for the power leaks that lead to our losing control of our time. The audit helps us get to the whys and motivators behind our loss of control.

10. Before the audit, take some time to review the "Holes in the Fence" that you listed in chapter 4. Which of these personal issues would you guess are contributing the most to your loss of time and energy?

DOING THE AUDIT PART ONE:
IDENTIFY WHAT YOU CARE ABOUT (VALUES, VISION, MISSION, AND GOALS)

Before you get to the mechanics of doing your audit, you must identify and clearly define your values, vision, mission, and goals.

Values

Values are what matter to us the most. They shape who we are and who we will become. The actions and behaviors of a person or organization are an expression of their values. In a sense, values are the DNA of the emerging you, your organization, your family, or whatever you are involved in and influence.

11. From the following list of values, rate (1–5, 5 being of utmost importance) those that are most important to you. This list is not complete, so feel free to add other values that you hold dear.

Ranking	General Values	Ranking	Character Values
	God		Honesty
	Family		Integrity
	Close friends		Love
	Health		Hope
	Recreation		Courage
	Relaxation		Faithfulness
	Emotional growth and intelligence		Freedom
	Intellectual growth		Loyalty
	Education		Justice
	Career growth		Forgiveness
	Financial growth		Excellence
	Spirituality		Communication
	Giving		Mercy
	Service		Tolerance
	Faith		Trust
			Wisdom
			Patience

Now look back at those values you ranked highest. Why did you choose them?

As you consider your life in light of the life-shaping values you selected, what do you learn about yourself and your life?

In Psalm 119:127, David reveals one of his most important life-shaping values, his value for God's ways: "I love your commands more than gold, more than pure gold."

12. As you think about your values, how well do you think they align with God's ways and the things that he values?

Which of your values put you in conflict with God's values?

Vision

Your vision is the picture of what you want the future to look like. A vision captures your dreams and lifts your heart to build something of great value. Whether it is for your company or for your personal life, a vision is key to getting where you want to go. Without a vision, we flounder and become the result of whatever forces prevail upon us. The power of a vision is so essential to life that Proverbs 29:18 (KJV) uses strong words to describe the result of such floundering: "Where there is no vision, the people perish."

13. How much time have you spent thinking about your vision for the different aspects of your life—career, family, personal life?

How would you put your vision—your picture of who you want to be, or what you want some part of your life to be—into words?

How do you feel about owning your vision? Does it seem possible to you?

Mission

Your mission is action-oriented. It is a more specific description of why you exist and what you will do to bring your vision to reality. Google's mission statement, for example, is action-oriented and keeps them on track: "Organize the world's information and make it universally accessible and useful." This simple statement provides a clear boundary for what the organization does and doesn't do.

14. What is your personal mission?

What is your professional mission?

How well do these personal and professional statements identify why you do what you do?

To what extent are these statements simple and narrow enough to keep you focused on actions that lead to your desired result?

Goals

Goals give direction, establish deadlines, and organize effort in a focused direction. They provide more specific boundaries and structure for how time and energy are spent. They are measurable and have a time line attached to them. They force you to drill down and get it done. In order to fulfill your vision and accomplish your mission, goals can—and probably need to be—short-term, medium-term, and long-term: lose ten pounds, finish a degree, become a senator.

15. Is establishing goals for your life a new concept to you, or are you a practiced goal-setter?

How would you rate your success in reaching your goals?

What have you accomplished (or do you hope to accomplish) by establishing goals?

Many people cannot entertain the thought that God would actually desire for them to fulfill their goals and dreams.

16. What role does faith play in your goals?

The psalmist writes, "Delight yourself in the LORD and he will give you the desires of your heart" (Psalm 37:4).

17. What is your reaction to this verse?

18. Write down objective, measurable short-term, medium-term, and long-term goals for both your personal and professional life. Be sure to include a time line for each!

DOING THE AUDIT PART TWO: LOG YOUR TIME

The time log is the tedious and most difficult part of the audit for some people to do. You may find that you resist actually logging your time. You may feel that you already know where your time is going, or that the time log won't reveal much. But remember, you are probably more subjective than you realize, and the only way to get a real accounting is to do a real accounting. So, commit to keeping an actual log as if you were going to bill for your time. After all, you are paying for how you spend your time: you pay for it with your life!

Step One

Choose a period of time—a week, two weeks, a month—that you think will give you a real picture of how you spend your time. For people with a pretty fixed schedule and routine, the accounting period can be shorter. For those with mixed activities, it may need to be longer. Next, log your time in thirty-minute increments and write down all of your activities during that time. Use ruled paper, a day calendar, whatever works best for you.

Remember, this requires no thought, analysis, or tweaking; it a is simple accounting of how you spend your time.

Step Two

Tally your time. Look for the themes and categories of where your time is going. In percentages, record below and on the next page what you discover. For example:

- 30 percent: taking calls that do not relate to my stated objectives
- 25 percent: in meetings that do not further my real agenda
- 40 percent: on operations when I need to be spending my time on vision and key relationships

Time Percentage	Activity	Disconnect, If Any (see p. 73)

Time Percentage	Activity	Disconnect, If Any (see p. 73)

Step Three

Let your audit talk to you about who (or what) is really in charge of your life. Identify the disconnects and seek to understand them. In other words, compare your time percentages with your stated values, vision, mission, and goals, noting the discrepancies. Answering the following questions will help:

Which areas can you identify that consume significant amounts of time and energy but have little or no relation to your values, vision, mission, or goals?

What overall percentage of your life is "on target," and how do you feel about that?

Delve further into the "whys" behind the disconnects. How do they happen?

What pulls you off task and which specific personal issues or power drains cause you to lose control?

What will you do to address these issues?

Step Four

Get an accountability and support system in place to help you realign your activities. If you are doing this study with a group, discuss how you can help each other. If you are not in a group that can provide the kind of support you need, who will you contact for help, accountability, and support?

Step Five

Figure out what new rules you need to have in place in order to live up to your accountability relationships and to keep the power drains from happening. List those new rules to live by here:

Remember, this book is about your entire life. Although you may have only done the audit on one aspect of your life, such as work, it may be helpful to do the audit on your personal life as well in order to create the one-life that you desire.

PRAYER

Dear God, this is hard. I acknowledge that my time really is my life, and also that it is difficult to be a good steward of it. As the Bible says, I really do "miss the mark" at times. Please help me to form the values, vision, mission, and goals that truly reflect who I am and the life you desire for me. Give me the courage and the healing I need to live according to the goals that will bring the vision for my life to reality. Help me as I take each step forward. Amen.

six

The Laws of Boundaries

The ten laws of boundaries are the principles you can use to make decisions about the people and situations you experience so that you can make the choices that enable you to live out your values.

One way to live life is to go along and figure out each problem as if it is unique. You face a problem in a relationship or at work, deal with it, hopefully fix it, and move on. Then you run into another problem and do it all over again. Each time you try to figure out what to do and work your way through it, often with much confusion and angst.

Another way to live is to see problems as examples of principles that are being violated. By viewing life in this way, you do not have to flounder each and every time you face a problem with a person or at work. You immediately recognize the principle being violated and, by focusing on the principle, you can know what to do pretty quickly. That is not to say that resolution is always easy, but it is much simpler.

The laws of boundaries are the principles that govern boundaries in relationships and work. If you know them, you will be able to step into situations and more quickly figure out what is wrong and what to do. Remember the goals of boundaries discussed in chapter 3? Boundaries give us the ability to do the following:

- Experience ourselves as separate and differentiated from others.
- Contain destruction and keep it from spreading.
- Define ourselves and know who we are.
- Set limits when needed.
- Possess and live out values.
- Have self-control and thereby be free and autonomous.

By applying the laws of boundaries, you are better able to make decisions about people and situations and figure out why some situations are askew. As a result, you will be more able to develop the abilities that boundaries provide.

1. In what ways have you been solving problems and making decisions as if each situation is unique rather than by seeking resolution to the principle being violated?

What differences might you expect to see in your life if you were to consistently apply the laws of boundaries in your relationships and in the workplace?

How do you feel about the potential for making that kind of change in your life?

LAW #1: THE LAW OF SOWING AND REAPING

According to this principle, the person who is doing a given behavior is the one who should be reaping the consequences of it, good or bad. This principle makes logical, common sense, but it is often violated in families, friendships, and among co-workers. In many situations someone is not pulling his or her weight, is acting irresponsibly, or is being hurtful, but that individual does not suffer the consequences. Instead, other people suffer the consequences and the one who is misbehaving is unlikely to change until he or she feels the consequences. The result is dysfunction, demotivation, and poor results.

God has designed an ordered universe in which there is cause and effect. One of the ways that behavior is ordered is by making sure that the person who is causing the problem is the one who feels the effects. When we violate this created order, we have disorder. So the law of sowing and reaping, which could also be called the law of natural consequences, is about making sure the right person feels the right consequence. One practical way to think about this principle is to ask, "Who did this and who should pay?" or "Who did this and who should get paid?"

2. In which relationships or situations have you seen the law of sowing and reaping violated? What were the results?

In each of these examples, who do you think was responsible to give consequences to the person, and why do you think he or she did not?

3. If there is a situation in your life in which this law is being violated and where you or someone you care about is suffering because another person is being allowed to behave in a destructive way without consequences, how should it be remedied, and who is responsible to do so?

LAW #2: THE LAW OF RESPONSIBILITY FOR AND TO

This principle says that you are responsible *for* yourself, and *to* others. There is nothing wrong with helping another person. Helping others is one of the foundations of relationship. But this principle identifies the lines as to whether you are helping them to do what they should be doing, and thus empowering them, or if you are doing for them what they should be doing for themselves.

This law reminds us that if we are trying to take responsibility and control for another person's life, choices, behaviors, etc., that we will be frustrated and so will they. It also reminds us that we have responsibilities to help each other but to do so without crossing the line of doing for others what they have to do for themselves.

4. When have you tried to take responsibility for another person's life in some way and tried to control what you could not control? What were the results?

When have you done for someone what that person should have been doing for himself or herself? What were the results for you and for that person?

What might you have done to be helpful *to* the individuals in these situations without crossing the line and being responsible *for* the individuals?

We cannot control another person's behaviors or choices, but we can act responsibly *to* them: we can confront, set limits, encourage, offer help, etc. But it is up to the person to do what he or she is going to do with the help or feedback that we provide.

5. With which person or in which situation that you face do you need to act responsibly *to* someone by confronting, setting limits, encouraging, offering to help, etc.?

If you are hesitant to fulfill your responsibility *to* that person, what is holding you back?

Where is the line between being responsible *to* that person and being responsible *for* that person, and how will you hold to it?

6. Jesus says, "If your brother sins against you, go and show him his fault, just between the two of you. If he listens to you, you have won your brother over" (Matthew 18:15). What does this verse say about your responsibility?

LAW #3: THE LAW OF POWER

God designed us to have power over ourselves, to have the power of self-control — the power to choose, to think, to act, to feel, to be self-directed, and the like. The law of power gives us only the ability to control ourselves, not the ability to control others. But sometimes we lose control of ourselves, thus losing the only power we have. This is what we call a "power drain."

Power drains happen when we give to others the power to determine who we are, what we think, what we want, and how we feel. You may know someone (perhaps that person is you) who loses power when in relationship with a certain person(s). It is as if the person loses control of himself or herself and gives the other person the ability to "make" them feel or behave a certain way. The law of power is about getting back in control of yourself so that others cannot "make" you feel crummy or do things that you do not want to do.

7. When have you witnessed a person giving up their own power to some other person? What were the results?

8. When have you given up your power to another person?

Why did you give up your power?

What were the results?

9. If you are in a power-drain situation right now, what steps are you willing to take to reclaim your power?

LAW #4: THE LAW OF RESPECT

When we find out that we have the power to choose and to say no to people's demands or irresponsible behavior, it is liberating. We love to be free. But we are not so fast to love the flip side of freedom: respecting other people's freedom. We like it when people do what we want them to do, but the reality is we sometimes have difficulty accepting other people's no or choices that we do not want them to make.

The law of respect is the same principle expressed in the Golden Rule: "Do to others as you would have them do to you" (Luke 6:31). If you are going to be an integrated person who is in control of yourself, you must not only command respect but must respect the boundaries of others. You must treat them in the way you want to be treated.

Sometimes living according to the law of respect is difficult because people make self-destructive choices. But, just as God sets us free to make our own choices and suffer the consequences, we must do the same. This does not mean that we do not confront or try to influence someone to make better choices. It does mean that, ultimately, just as Jesus did with the rich young ruler (see Matthew 19:22), we have to allow others to choose what they choose.

10. When do you find it most difficult to respect someone else's boundaries when they say no to you?

If there is a relationship right now in which you are finding it difficult to receive the other person's no, why is it so hard?

11. In what ways do the following verses guide you in practicing the law of respect?

   Philippians 2:3 Do nothing out of selfish ambition or vain conceit, but in humility consider others better than yourselves.

   Philippians 2:4 Each of you should look not only to your own interests, but also to the interests of others.

Some of the most difficult times to respect another person's boundaries and choices is when they choose against our advice and continue to do something destructive.

12. When have you experienced this and what was it like?

13. With which person in your life do you need to accept their decision not to do the right thing and allow them to suffer the consequences? What makes it hard for you to respect their boundary?

LAW #5: THE LAW OF MOTIVATION

Remember the feeling you had the last time you did something because you wanted to? There was energy, chemical reactions that went off in your head that you felt throughout your entire being. You did not have to make yourself do it. You just did. That is truly an awesome experience.

The reason such an experience is so great is that it comes from your heart being "at one" with your decision. It is a full-hearted yes! It leads to "cheerful giving" as the Bible says. This does not mean that we actually like doing all that is involved in our choice, but it means that we like the choice itself. For example, when a medical student stays up thirty-six hours in a row as a resident, he or she probably is not enjoying that shift. But the bigger choice of training to become a doctor was most likely a positive choice, not one done from a negative motivation. That "wholeheartedness" of the resident's choice is the same kind of motivation that Jesus had when choosing to go through the agony of the cross. It was something he wanted to do, not something he was forced into.

The law of motivation is about getting to the essence of why we do what we do. It is about realizing that no one is making you do whatever you are doing, but you are choosing it for some motivation of your own. So are you choosing out of a good purpose? Or are you choosing out of fear, compulsion, or some lack of freedom to say no? Many times such choices come from being manipulated by someone rather than from a true expression of your values and talents.

I think 2 Corinthians 9:7 — "Each man should give what he has decided in his heart to give, not reluctantly or under compulsion, for God loves a cheerful giver" — speaks to our motivations as well as to our giving.

14. What does it mean to you to have a wholehearted motivation that is not forced or hindered by reluctance or compulsion?

15. If you ever have acted reluctantly because you were being forced or manipulated, what was that like and what were the results for you?

    In which relationships or situations do you feel pressure either from another person or inside yourself to give of yourself where you do not really want to?

    If you have not examined your motivations in this situation, now would be a good time to do so. Why are you doing what you are doing?

16. How do you tell the difference between giving "against your will" and enduring painful sacrifice that is good and positively motivated?

LAW #6: THE LAW OF EVALUATION OF PAIN

Just because someone is screaming doesn't mean that something bad is happening. When a toddler gets put in time-out, the noise can be deafening. When you say no to a control freak, it may not be pretty. When you set limits with an irresponsible person, he may protest. But just because someone cries "hurt" doesn't mean you are doing something harmful.

When someone protests against what we are doing, we have to evaluate the pain to see if it is valid. If we are harming or injuring someone, that is not good. But to make choices that might be difficult for someone, or cause the pain of discipline is not a bad thing. Discipline, the Bible reminds us, is not supposed to be pleasant: "No discipline seems pleasant at the time, but painful. Later on, however, it produces a harvest of righteousness and peace for those who have been trained by it" (Hebrews 12:11).

17. In which situation in your life does the principle expressed in this verse apply?

18. How do you handle a person who is irresponsible, controlling, or just selfish and "screams" when you have boundaries in your life?

In what ways would you like to change your current response to that person?

What is keeping you from making those changes?

LAW #7: THE LAW OF PROACTIVITY

The principle expressed by the law of proactivity is to be a cause instead of a result. Being proactive means to anticipate what is needed and to do it before you suffer the consequences of not doing it. It is to become part of the solution instead of just reacting to whatever life hands you. For example, proactive people who are in debt pick up the phone and call the credit card company to work out a settlement instead of waiting for their credit to be ruined.

To own your life means that you see what is needed and take action. That way, you are creating the life you want. You are making your vision a reality as opposed to accepting whatever life brings your way.

19. Which threads of passive reacting can you identify in specific situations in your life?

What has been the result of reacting to a result rather than acting to cause a result?

Which actions could you have taken in these situations to be more proactive, and what better result would you likely have experienced?

20. In which current situation or relationship would you do well to pick up the phone and take the first step to cause something good to happen?

What keeps you from doing that?

LAW #8: THE LAW OF ENVY

Envy defines what is good as what we do not have. When envy dominates a person, he or she is looking over the fence at another person's yard and thinking that the other person's position, relationships, status, or possessions would bring happiness. People who are dominated by envy feel that the really valuable things in life are the ones that they do not have, but once they have those things they immediately lose their value. So, the envious person never feels grateful or content. There is always a "next thing" or relationship that he or she will want.

The law of envy says that instead of looking over the fence to find out what would make you happy, you take ownership of your own yard and look at your own heart to see what good things you truly desire. If you are motivated by a real desire instead of envy, you have greater self-control and are poised to take responsibility for going and getting what you desire. Desire means ownership and responsibility. Otherwise, it is just envy: wanting what you do not have and always not having enough.

Envy is in opposition to the wisdom of Proverbs 14:30: "A heart at peace gives life to the body, but envy rots the bones."

21. Describe the ways in which envy robs you of peace and drains your life.

In which particular areas — relationships, possessions, or status — do you struggle with envy?

What has been the result when you have pursued something out of envy and then attained it?

God knows how destructive envy is, and the Bible cautions us to "rid yourselves of all malice and all deceit, hypocrisy, envy, and slander of every kind" (1 Peter 2:1).

22. For which areas of envy do you need (and want) God's help to get rid of?

23. Which desires can you feel good about and actively pursue because they really come from your heart and not from envy?

What resistance do you have to owning these true desires and pursuing them?

LAW #9: THE LAW OF ACTIVITY

The law of activity is a cousin of the law of proactivity, but it is a little different. Proactivity is about addressing issues first instead of reacting to outside forces. Activity is about realizing that nothing happens if you do not do something. As Newton observed in his first law, an object at rest will tend to stay at rest unless acted upon by an external force. Translated into life, this means that the results you get are because of what you do, or do not do.

This principle reflects the way God designed us—not to be passive and just wait for life to give us things but to go out and get them. To illustrate this, consider the wise observation of Proverbs 13:4: "The sluggard craves and gets nothing, but the desires of the diligent are fully satisfied." Unless you do something different, nothing is going to be different. If you want to experience a different reality, you will to have to do something to make things different.

24. What does Proverbs 13:4 say to you about pursuing the desires of your heart?

The law of activity is also related to our faith. The Bible tells us that faith without works is dead, so to step out and do something is part of what it means to live out our faith in God. Hebrews 10:38 is very clear: "But my righteous one will live by faith. And if he shrinks back, I will not be pleased with him."

25. What does this verse say to you about faith and taking action in a situation in your life (perhaps a situation that you have been putting up with for too long)?

What has been keeping you from taking action in this situation?

What is the first step you can take to get moving?

LAW #10: THE LAW OF EXPOSURE

The law of exposure is about exposing your boundaries and bringing them into the light so that others know where you stand. When people expose their boundaries, they are open and clear. They take the issue right to the person with whom they have a conflict. They tell others what they want, like, dislike, expect, or what displeases them. As the Bible says, they "speak the truth in love."

Direct, open, honest, firm, and kind boundaries that are communicated directly make every kind of relationship better. Unless you are a spy or a terrorist trying to sneak in under the radar, get it out in the open.

26. What has been your experience in being clear about your boundaries and communicating them directly?

27. What has been the outcome when you were not clear about your boundaries?

If there is someone in your life right now with whom you are afraid to be direct and clear, what is the reason for your fear? What are you willing to do about it?

Honesty and clarity in our relationships is a recurring theme in the Bible. Consider, for example, the instruction in the following verses:

Ephesians 4:25   Therefore each of you must put off falsehood and speak truthfully to his neighbor, for we are all members of one body.

Matthew 18:15   If your brother sins against you go and show him his fault, just between the two of you. If he listens to you, you have won your brother over.

28. How do these verses help you understand the importance of clearly exposing your boundaries in your personal and professional relationships?

29. What changes do you want to make in how you expose your boundaries?

PRAYER

Dear God, thank you, first of all, that you are a God of order and have established laws that govern the universe; and thank you also that you have made those known to us. I confess there are ways I have not applied those laws to certain situations and relationships. Help me to see where they apply, and give me the knowledge and ability to apply them. Amen.

seven

You and Your Words

Our relationship with certain words is built into our character through our early experiences in significant relationships. It can result in a pattern of not saying what we want, what we think, or what we will or won't do.

Most of us have thought, "Whatever possessed me to say yes to this in the first place? Why didn't I just say no?" Or, after negotiating a deal, we may think, "Why didn't I ask for _____? I could kick myself!" However, if you have these thoughts often, it reveals that you and your words are not on the same page.

You desire one outcome, but your words
take you to a different one.

The idea that you have a relationship with words may be new to you. But in the depths of people's souls, where true behavior originates, there is a real relationship with certain words. The nature of that relationship dictates a lot of what happens in people's lives. If the relationship is good, they are able to use certain words to create and maintain a healthy structure and boundaries. But if they do not get along well with those words, then structure and boundaries are compromised and their lives become fragmented.

The essence of this concept is this: you need certain words at certain times, and if you are not free to use them, then you will not be able to do what is needed. Our goal is to find out which of the important words you might have trouble with, and to reclaim them.

1. With which words might you have a relationship problem, such as being unable to use them when you need to or using them too much?

2. With which words do you sense a conflict or disconnect between what you deeply desire and what you actually say?

INTERNALIZATIONS AND PATTERNS

Think about people you know (perhaps even yourself) who routinely find themselves in some situation —an activity, relationship, scheduling conflict, or problem—they do not want to be in. The reason is not that they fail to say no once or twice: they basically never say no. Their choices are rarely about what they want or don't want. Their choices usually are about their conflicted relationship with the word "no." They reach deep inside in hopes of finding "no," but it eludes them.

Or, think of the person on your team who you know you cannot send into a meeting to ask for the moon. This person just can't pull the trigger and ask for what he or she wants. As a result, people like this rarely get out of life what they desire and oftentimes don't even get what they need. In contrast, other people go into a meeting, ask for the moon, and get it.

These situations illustrate patterns of internalizations. It is not so much that one person wanted something and the other did not. It was more that one person had developed a pattern of being able to ask and the other had not. We all have patterns of ability or inability when it comes to certain words, and we need to reclaim those words so we can use them when we need to. Our task is twofold: to discover if there are patterns with words that are limiting our ability to use them, and to figure out where those patterns come from and change them.

3. Which results of being unable to use certain words well have you seen in your workplace? In your personal life?

THE WORD AUDIT

You've already done a time audit. Now we are going to apply a similar audit to your relationship to words. To see a pattern and observe it is to begin to change. It is the first step toward developing new patterns and having new experiences.

Remember, your use of words has a lot to do with your ability to have boundaries that enable you to:

- Experience yourself as separate and differentiated from others.
- Contain destruction and keep it from spreading.
- Define yourself and know who you are.
- Set limits when needed.
- Possess and live out values.
- Have self-control and thereby be free and autonomous.

The strong connection between words and boundaries is affirmed in the wisdom of the Bible. Consider, for example, what the following verses say in terms of how our words are connected to what we experience in life:

Proverbs 12:14   From the fruit of his lips a man is filled with good things as surely as the work of his hands rewards him.

Proverbs 13:2   From the fruit of his lips a man enjoys good things.

Proverbs 18:20   From the fruit of his mouth a man's stomach is filled; with the harvest from his lips he is satisfied.

Proverbs 18:21   The tongue has the power of life and death, and those who love it will eat its fruit.

4. In your own words, how would you express the connection between your words and what you experience in life?

5. Select one or more of the abilities from the boundaries list (bullet points above) and name a time that you had to speak out to make those things happen.

6. Select one or more examples from the same list and name a time that you found yourself unable to say the words you needed to say to make those things happen.

Why do you think you couldn't say what you needed to say?

THE WORDS

Now let's take a closer look at the ways certain words might affect your ability to experience the above outcomes.

"I Think ..."

If you cannot say "I think," then you will not experience yourself as a separate person, fully differentiated from others. As a result, you will lose important aspects to your functioning, including the ability to self-direct, stand firm against difficult people, feel okay when others put you down, persuade and influence the direction of a conversation, deal, or team, and so on.

Telling others what you think defines who you are. It differentiates you from them, from their opinions, and from their beliefs. It also expresses the power you were designed to have. So get the words out and begin sharing what's in that head of yours!

7. What is your pattern of saying what you think?

If speaking your mind does not come easily for you, why?

8. In which current relationship or situation do you need to speak your mind more directly than you are doing, and how will you do that?

"I Won't ..."

If you find it difficult to say "I won't" or "no," then you are subject to being drawn into many destructive patterns — everything from simply overextending yourself to downright illegalities. Even in good situations, you might agree to do things you don't want to do. In difficult situations, you have to know the bottom line of what you won't do and be able to draw the line so you don't end up on the wrong end of an agreement. If you can't do that, your boundary lines will get moved past where you want them to be.

9. How well do you say what you "won't" do?

If it is hard for you, and you tend to keep silent, what are the results and how have they hurt you?

Why do you think you allow this to happen?

How would you like the results to be different, and what do you need to say in order to make them different?

"I Want …"

If saying the words "I want" is tough for you, then you are going to find yourself getting leftovers in many situations, and not getting the performance out of others that you need to move your projects forward. In a very real sense, you get what you ask for.

If you have trouble saying "I want," it might help to realize that even God wants to know what we want: "You do not have, because you do not ask God" (James 4:2).

10. To what extent does James 4:2 encourage you to ask for what you want in your relationships with God and with people?

11. In which situations or with which people is asking for what you want most difficult, and why?

What one thing would you take the risk and ask for in these situations or with these people?

"I Will ..."

The more what you say you will do is lined up with your desires, the closer you are to living one life, the life you desire. Unfortunately, sometimes we lack alignment between what we desire and what we say we will do. We say we "will" when it is the last thing we want to do. We then are not giving of ourselves but are giving in. We say the words "I will" when we cannot resist the pressure (internal or external), yet we know that we may or may not follow through (and if we do follow through, we may resent it).

12. What is your pattern with the words "I will"? Do you tend to say it more than you mean or want to, or do you avoid saying it when you really want to?

13. Name a situation in which you wish you had not said "I will."

Why do you think you did that, and in which situations are you doing that now?

14. Name a situation in which you wish you had jumped in and said "I will."

Why didn't you do that, and in which situations are you doing that now?

"Yes" and "No"

Most of our uses of "yes" and "no" are pretty obvious, and they are big direction setters in life. What we say yes to is where we are headed and what we say no to keeps us going in a particular direction. Yes joins us and no separates us. Therefore, they play huge roles in defining who we are and what we end up doing and not doing.

The word "no" is especially relevant to boundaries and structure. "No" defines limits. Saying no reflects our ability to set limits and define ourselves. Saying yes reflects our ability to join and agree with people and things that they desire.

15. How effective are you in saying yes and no?

Is one harder for you to say than the other? Why, and in which situations or with which people?

16. Name a situation when either saying yes or no could have made a big difference and describe the consequences.

What would you do to respond differently if you faced a similar situation today?

"I Don't Know"

The ability to say "I don't know" can be a powerful, self-defining act. Whenever a person tries to fake it, or feels as if he or she has to, there is a crack in the foundation that will reveal itself in some way. To not fake it and be real requires taking a very strong stance that says, "I am secure enough in who I am to be who I am." Often business situations are so full of ego and posturing that a real, secure person stands out as a towering figure among the fakes. Admitting what you do not know solidifies that what you do assert is actually true. And if you are good enough in what you do know, what you don't know won't kill you.

17. When do you have trouble saying "I don't know"?

18. Do you think admitting that you don't know would be helpful or hurtful to you in the big picture? Why, and with whom?

What would have to change within you to find the freedom to admit that you sometimes don't know the answer?

"I Was Wrong"

To avoid taking responsibility for one's side of something is one of the ultimate killers in any relationship, personal or professional. In fact, it makes real relationship impossible. When one person refuses to own something, the relationship has hit a wall. True relatedness ends and managing one another begins. "Lawyering up" or not admitting wrong might be a good strategy in court, but it should not be your strategy in life, either professionally or personally. Admitting wrong helps us solve problems, get better, and builds hope and trust with those to whom we relate.

19. In which situations or with which people is it difficult for you to admit when you are wrong?

What are the results of not admitting your responsibility?

20. How do you think the message of James 5:16 — "Confess your [faults] to each other ... so that you may be healed" — would help you admit your wrongs in these situations?

Do you think there are times to admit wrongs and times not to admit them? Why?

"When You ..."

There is also the opposite side of admitting your own fault. That is when someone else, not you, is on the wrong side of a behavior or mistake. This statement is about acknowledging that someone else is doing something you do not like, are uncomfortable with, or is flat-out wrong. This is about confronting others when they are wrong or when you want them to own something. It is one of the most important boundary structures there is, especially in containing destruction, remaining separate from other people's problems, and limiting someone else's toxic dynamics from taking over your yard. It is also one of the most, if not the most, difficult relationships with words that many people have.

21. How difficult is it for you to tell other people about their problem behavior?

When have you had difficulty doing this and why?

22. What important guidance do the following verses offer in confronting the wrong behavior of others?

Matthew 18:15 If your brother sins against you, go and show him his fault, just between the two of you. If he listens to you, you have won your brother over.

Galatians 6:1 Brothers, if someone is caught in a sin, you who are spiritual should restore him gently.

23. If you face a person or a situation now where it is difficult for you to confront wrongdoing, what do you need to do differently?

FREE SPEECH IN THE FUTURE

Reestablishing a good relationship with these important words is a process. You will want to write down or share your thoughts and plans for each of these steps as you move forward:

Take this idea seriously. Do not assume that you are immune from having a characteristic pattern of using or not using certain words. Talk these things through with someone—a coach, friend, or counselor. Get some insight, and get past this. You need free speech to be a part of your life. It is a cornerstone of your personal power that affects everything you do.

Play the movie of your life, past and present. Identify patterns that cause you to repeatedly say some words but also refrain from saying others. What is consistently missing in your life that could be present if you could say the things you need to say? What are the fears, hurts, or relationships that brought those patterns about? In what ways are people from your past still inside your head, controlling your use of words?

Seek out new experiences that develop new patterns. You will grow and change only as you have different experiences and different outcomes. Attend some skills-building workshops, join a group, practice what you know you need to do with someone who holds you accountable. Write down what you need to say in difficult situations and role-play the conversation with a friend.

Make this a team exercise. Talking about the issue of free speech is one of the best things a team can do together. Get this all out on the table and talk about how the team and the culture of the company work around these words.

Get a coach or someone to help you. Part of the process of change involves opening up our performance to a wise, experienced person who can observe us and speak to our patterns and practices. Today, more than ever, executive and leadership coaching is readily available. Find a coach, invest the time and money in your growth, and reclaim your ability to speak the words you need to speak to get the results you desire.

Remember, as Proverbs tells us, we do experience the fruit of our words. Words are important and God has given you the ability to use them in the service of all things good. Now it is your turn to take control of your words and develop a good relationship with them.

PRAYER

Dear God, thank you for creating me in your image with the ability to speak. I confess to you that I have not always used my words well. I acknowledge that some of that comes from my own fear and some of it comes out of experiences that I have had that have made it difficult for me. For my part of that, I confess to you my wrong and ask you to help me do better. For the part that comes from hurtful experiences that need to be healed and strengthened, I ask for your help. Restore in me the ability to use the right words at the right times to accomplish the right things. Amen.

eight

Make the "No-Choice" Choices First

Certain choices in life are not really an option. The paradox is that eliminating some choices as options is, in itself, a choice.

If you are like most people, you either have a mortgage or pay rent. When the first of the month rolls around, you pay it. You don't think about whether or not you are going to do it, nor do you put it off and spend the money on other things. You choose not to have a choice about paying the mortgage or rent. You know that if you don't write that check, you are going to lose your home. Either foreclosure or eviction awaits you if you don't pay, so you pay it first, before you spend the money on anything else.

1. To get in the mindset of the no-choice choices, what are some things that you do "automatically" without experiencing them as choices, and why do you do them?

Paying your mortgage or rent is a no-choice experience. You choose to do it without even considering that you have any other choice. The consequences of not paying are so great that it is not even an option. But in other areas of life, such as how we spend our resources of time and energy, we do not think that way. We often spend those resources on less important things and have little left over to spend on the things that are vital to our real values, mission, and goals. So you have work to do if you want to spend your time and energy in the same way you spend your rent or mortgage money: on the most vital things first.

THE BIG ROCKS

You may have heard the illustration of the professor who asked his class how many rocks he could fit in a jar already half-filled with pebbles. By dumping out the pebbles, putting the rocks in the jar first, then allowing the pebbles to fill the nooks and crannies, he showed that more of what is important fits into a given space when the important things (rocks) are put in first and the less important things (pebbles) are used to fill the space that is left. Life is like that too. All of the activities in life are not equal. Some activities are rocks and some are pebbles. The key is to know the difference and to put the rocks—the most important ones—in first.

This isn't easy for us to do. We often need reminders to separate the rocks from the pebbles and to put the important rocks in first. Consider, for example, Jesus' gentle reminder to Martha: "Martha, Martha . . . you are worried and upset about many things, but only one thing is needed. Mary has chosen what is better, and it will not be taken away from her" (Luke 10:41 – 42).

2. What do you think Jesus might say to you about recognizing the one thing that is needed and separating the rocks from the pebbles in your life?

3. Which activities that get some of the best of your time and energy would you consider to be "rocks" and "choosing what is better"?

Which activities, if you really evaluated them in light of your values, mission, and goals, are really "pebbles"—even though they may be good activities in and of themselves?

On which "rocks" would you rather be spending that time and energy?

4. Which relationships that get the best of your time and energy would you consider to be "rocks" and "choosing what is better"?

What fruit do you receive in these relationships as a result?

If you evaluated your relationships in light of your values, mission, and goals, which ones would not deserve the best investment of your time and energy?

To which relationships do you want to give that time and energy instead?

VITAL VS. URGENT

Some of the most vital activities in life are not the most urgent activities. The word "vital" means that something is necessary to the maintenance of life. If you ignore vital activities, life cannot be maintained and death will occur. But vital activities often can be put aside temporarily while you do something non-vital, and you will feel no pain. But if you continue to ignore the vital activities, something will die.

5. What would you consider to be the vital activities in your life that need to get the no-choice expenditure of your time and energy? In the chart on pages 108–109, write down the vital activities for each area of life. Next, write down the urgent activites that have been receiving a higher priority of your time and energy than you would like. Finally, identify what you need to face in order to deal with the discrepancy, and reorder the activities you want to keep in accordance with their precedence.

		No-Choice Vital Activities	Urgent Activities That Get My Attention
AREAS OF LIFE	Personal		
	Professional		
	Emotional		
	Spiritual		
	Relational		

What I Need to Face	How I Want to Reorder These Activities

In light of the concept of the rocks and pebbles, the vital and the urgent, consider this advice from the Bible: "Remember this: whoever sows sparingly will also reap sparingly, and whoever sows generously will also reap generously" (2 Corinthians 9:6).

6. What does this verse say to you about sowing not just money but your time and energy in order to gain the things that you have deemed to be most important?

Doing the important things first is a hallmark of good character, and it is a struggle for all of us. As the saying goes, the road to hell is paved with good intentions. Isn't it time to get off the road of good intentions and put your values into practice by making some no-choice choices in the vital areas of your life?

7. Which rocks would you like to place in your life first, and where are they going to go? Some people have found helpful categories to be a good starting point. Feel free to choose from this list and come up with your own:

Structured family time. It might include things like a weekly family meeting or certain meals when everyone will be there.

   My family-time rock:

Date night. A date night that is in the schedule—a rock that does not get moved—has a much higher probability of actually happening than just finding time to go out.

   My date-night rock:

One-on-one parenting time. An example would be a scheduled restaurant breakfast with your teenager, or some other regular activity.

My parenting-time rock:

Scheduled exercise time. Exercise time cannot be a when-I-get-around-to-it event. People who exercise regularly do exactly that—regularly. It is not just time that they have left over from other things.

My exercise rock:

Automatic savings. Make it a rule to pay yourself first. If savings are first and discretionary income comes after savings, you will save. If you spend before saving, spending will always win.

My savings rock:

Planned vacations. If your vacation time is scheduled ahead, you will order and organize work around it. You will be more efficient.

My vacation rock:

Regular team time. Teams who have structured times to get together will get together. Those who don't tend to pass in the night and always play catch-up.

My team-time rock:

Regular friend time. With some friends you can get together as time allows, but you might want to have "rock time" with your closest friends.

My friend-time rock:

Scheduled recreational time. Is there a regular time that everyone knows you are going to be doing something that re-creates you?

My recreational rock:

Scheduled spiritual time. Make a regular appointment to devote time specifically to your spiritual life.

My spiritual rock:

Routine participation in a support group, accountability group, or regular appointments with a mentor, coach, or therapist. You will be more grounded in life if you are regularly involved with a support system than if you depend only on yourself.

   My support rock:

Growth-oriented activities. Some professions have continuing education requirements that help their workers to keep growing "at the job." Treat your own growth in the same way.

   My personal-growth rock:

PRAYER

Dear God, it is so easy to get sidetracked by good, and urgent, but not vital activities and relationships. I confess that I do that and ask you to help me to see exactly where I do it. Please help me to make the changes in my time and energy that I need to make. Help me to do a thorough soul search and get on track in the key areas in which I need to spend the best of who I am and what I have. Amen.

nine

Follow the Misery and Make a Rule

Getting a handle on the misery that creates time and energy drains in your life and making a rule to prevent them is like finding a gold mine.

Rules are often made following some sort of bad occurrence. When people prove themselves unable to do something responsibly, that practice is no longer allowed. Rules are instituted to keep the order that people are not keeping themselves. They limit and protect. Rules can be positive in nature as well, requiring the practice of good behaviors, such as continuing education to maintain a professional license.

1. What is your general reaction to the concept of rules, and to what extent do you consider rules to be a positive or negative influence on your life?

PERSONAL POLICIES

Externally imposed rules can be negative or positive — the "thou shalt nots" and the "thou shalts." But what about you personally? What are the non-universal rules that you make just for yourself — the rules that dictate how to be you?

These rules have to do with areas of your life in which you are morally, legally, and ethically free to engage, but that you have found are not the best practices for you. No one would know if you broke the rules or engaged in the activities, but your life would not go as well if you did. By setting rules for yourself, you either limit or exert your personal freedom to make life better for you and to reach your business or personal objectives.

2. What are some personal rules or policies that you live by that are not moral universals but that you have found helpful for living your life?

How did you come to adopt these rules, and what has been the result?

The apostle Paul reflects the idea of establishing personal rules when he writes, " 'Everything is permissible for me' — but not everything is beneficial" (1 Corinthians 6:12). He makes it clear that there are practices in which he may be free to engage, but which may not be good for him to do. Our personal policies help us make rules that guide us away from things that are not beneficial to us, and toward things that are. They help us apply the wisdom of Proverbs 22:3: "A prudent man sees danger and takes refuge, but the simple keep going and suffer for it."

3. When you see practices or relationships in your life that are not beneficial to you, or may even be harmful to what is most important to you, what are you inclined to do?

4. What kind of rules might you establish for yourself to keep you from danger or suffering?

5. What kind of rules might you establish for yourself to help you focus on living the life you desire?

Rules are essential, but a word of caution is in order when it comes to them: life is not about rules! Jesus repeatedly reminded the Pharisees of this because they often put rules above life itself. What he said to them, "The Sabbath was made for people, not people for the Sabbath" (Mark 2:27 TNIV) is true for you as well. Rules are there to help you. The rules you make to help structure your life should serve you, not the other way around.

6. How do you know where to draw the line between a rule that is serving you well and one that has become too much of a master?

To live by learning what is profitable and what is not, and then adjusting our ways accordingly, is to practice what the Bible calls "wisdom." Some people spurn any idea of a "rule" or constraint on their "freedom" and continue to go about their destructive ways, never learning. The problem is, as Paul pointed out, all of our freedom is not always good for us. We can become trapped in our freedom. The paradox is, although rules limit you in some ways, they empower you in others. While they take away some freedom, they give you more freedom than you could ever have without them. Wisdom shows us when our freedom is good for us and when it isn't. But how do we go about making rules that give us self-control resulting in wise living?

FIND THE MISERY AND SET THE RULE

To figure out which rules we may need to implement, it is sometimes helpful to begin by "finding the misery." In other words, find the areas of life in which we are experiencing pain, distress, annoyance, or interference with the outcomes we desire.

Begin the process by examining any toxic relationships, energy drains, or random practices that continually happen (or do not happen) and result in some sort of misery in your life. Examine any other areas of misery that you can identify, and begin writing down new personal policies and rules that will keep you from the misery.

Toxic Relationships

Some people, for whatever reason, have the ability to make you miserable. By making a rule or two for yourself, you can keep yourself from a lot of misery. But remember, you cannot control the other person's toxic behavior, so the rule has to be for you, not for the other person.

7. Which key relationships are causing you misery, and what specific behaviors are the culprits?

Which rules for yourself would limit your exposure to that person's behavior and its impact on your life? (i.e., I will not be around that person if he is drinking; I will not talk one-on-one about that subject with that person.)

What are your fears in setting those rules for yourself, and what will those rules set you free to do or to enjoy?

Managing Your Energy for High Performance

"I don't have time" or "I don't have it in me" are two of the most uttered sentences that prevent people from accomplishing the life they desire. If the normal ebb and flow of the way you go about your work is ineffective, then you must find the misery and make a rule that will restore your productivity. Even a little rule can limit your freedom to make yourself miserable! So begin assessing your time and energy drains.

8. For which activities do you need your best energy?

When is your best energy available to you?

What rules could you set to preserve your best energy for your most demanding activities?

9. Which energy drains can you identify? (Be sure to include people as well as activities!)

What rules and physical practices could you establish to protect you from interference and energy loss? (i.e., I will not schedule a meeting or phone call with that draining person right before having to do something that requires me to be at 100 percent energy level.)

Random Practices

Rules are about learning from your experience and not enduring the same misery for longer than it takes to learn what is creating it. There may be many areas of life in which what you are doing is not giving you the results you desire. If so, it's time to look at each area and make the rules that will put you in control.

10. Which "little" things in your life (like taking a Blackberry on date night or having chips in the house) are having a negative impact on the life you desire?

For each of these, write down a personal rule that will give you self-control over the misery. Remember, these rules can be positive (what you will do for yourself) as well as negative (what you will no longer do).

Who can you ask to help you be accountable to your decision?

PRAYER

Dear God, thank you for introducing me to the idea of rules that can help keep me from misery. Help me to see the sources of my misery and to figure out some rules that will give me freedom to truly live. Help me to see which desires I have that may be helped by some personal rules, and give me the wisdom I need to figure out what those will be. Help me keep those rules, and when I fail or need to change them, help me with that as well. Amen.

Part Three

BOUNDARIES ON THE JOB

ten

Time, Space, and E-mail

E-mail has no door to close so you can focus on what is most important to you. So you have to create one.

As I mentioned in chapter 1, not that long ago people used to go "to" work and be "at" work in a very structured way. Work happened in a space, like an office, and for a specific period of time, such as 8:00 to 5:00. Work had boundaries of space and time so it could not invade your personal space and time after you left the office.

Not so anymore. The freedom that technology brings comes with a price. You are no longer protected from work and other people's agendas—whether at the office or away from it—unless you protect yourself. So the goal is to regain your protective boundaries of time and space, particularly from the invasion of technology and e-mail.

1. In what ways have you felt the pressure of technology invading your boundaries of time and space at home and at work?

How have you tried to deal with this problem, and how effective have you been?

WHAT CONTROLS YOUR TIME?

Our days and our time are important, and it is the work of wisdom to figure out how to control our time and use it effectively. In Ephesians 5:15 – 16, the apostle Paul tells us to use our time wisely, even as he acknowledges that the days in which we live can make that difficult. And in Romans 14:12, he adds that we will be held accountable to God for how we've lived, in other words, how we've spent our days.

So the big question is, "Who is in control of your time and space?" More specifically, who dictates how you use your time and what you will focus on next? Are you in control, or is your inbox in control? The question of who is in control is paramount, so let's take a look at how your time is controlled.

2. How would you describe your relationship with e-mail? Is it your servant, a tool that creates efficiency; is it a distraction; or is it more like a master that keeps you from doing what is most important?

3. Name specific examples of how e-mail interrupts you when you are doing what is most vital to you, either professionally or personally.

What do you think is the real cost of these interruptions?

Which practices at work or at home allow these interruptions to happen? Do you work, for example, with your inbox turned on, or do you feel you must respond immediately to every e-mail no matter what else you need to get done?

What ideas do you have for boundaries that would protect you from these interruptions?

CREATE YOUR OWN AGENDA

Obviously you cannot completely ignore your e-mail or other distractions of technology. Today they are how business gets done. However, it is important to think about how you can work with the technology. The first step is to make sure you are setting your agenda.

4. Think for a moment about the work you do every day. Who really is in charge of your agenda or the specific tasks on which you work? You, or your inbox?

5. Think through a typical work day. Who really is in charge of your time or when you do specific tasks? You or your e-mail?

6. Where do you see a need for increasing your control of your agenda and your time?

A good way of getting back in control of your time is to set specific daily and weekly objectives. Simply by asking yourself the question, "What would define a successful day for me?" and then setting an agenda to achieve that objective, is a very empowering practice. Give it a try:

7. Chart out what you need to accomplish to make this week a successful week for you. Then list the tasks you need to accomplish each day in order to make that happen.

To make this week a success, I will:

On Monday I will:

On Tuesday I will:

On Wednesday I will:

On Thursday I will:

On Friday I will:

PROTECT YOUR AGENDA

Setting your agenda is the easy part! The real challenge is to take control and protect those objectives by protecting your agenda. Ephesians 2:10 says there are good works that already have been planned by God and have been designed for you to accomplish. Your task is to walk in them. To do that, you have to be purposeful and in control of how you spend your time. That is the value of making a daily agenda and then protecting it.

So evaluate some of the protection strategies suggested in *The One-Life Solution.*

☐ *Close your e-mail program for a specific, blocked-out time period.*

8. How much could this help you?

How difficult would it be to implement this practice?

To what extent would the benefits outweigh the cost?

☐ *Assign a time for checking e-mail and voice mail and for returning calls.*

9. What would you gain by doing this?

What might you lose, and is that cost real or psychological?

☐ *Turn off the ringer on your phone.*

10. What would it be like to be "unavailable" to everything but your own agenda for a while?

What benefits to this practice can you see?

How would this practice move your agenda forward, or hinder your progress?

☐ *Create folders* (e.g., immediate action required, action required soon, no time required).

11. What does your inbox look like? (How many e-mails are there now?)

How much time do you waste finding the crucial items that require action?

What would make this system work better for you?

☐ *Close the door* ("A prudent man sees danger and takes refuge, but the simple keep going and suffer for it." — Proverbs 22:3).

12. Where is your space that is free from interruptions and power drains?

What time of day is the best time for you to create a space where all interruptions are kept on the other side of the door?

What are the most important things for you to focus on when you have protected time and space?

How much time do you need to spend in your protected time and space in order to be effective?

☐ *Sort e-mails by sender.*

13. How would this cleanup strategy help you?

Notice who you get the most e-mails from and evaluate how helpful those e-mails are. This may lead you to some helpful discussions or new ways of working with that person.

☐ *Ask yourself "who and why."*

14. Whose calls or e-mails take control of your mind, focus, and time?

Why should this person have that much access to you, and is there a power drain at work that allows them to gain control over your agenda? What about that person makes you afraid? (Remember: "Fear of man will prove to be a snare, but whoever trusts in the LORD is kept safe" – Proverbs 29:25.)

☐ *Are you addicted?* To remain true to our purposes, it is helpful to take a look at the purity of our work to ensure that we are not serving some type of idol. Second Peter 2:19 (TNIV) cautions us about the reality of idolatry: "for people are slaves to whatever has mastered them."

15. What does this verse say to you in light of not being able to get away from work? To what extent has work become your master?

To what degree may your work or some of the distractions that affect it be filling a spiritual, emotional, or relational void?

What happens when you try not to check e-mail or take some protected time away from it all? Do you get fidgety? Do you suspect that you are hiding from some internal reality?

Being purposeful and having a mission means that you are in control, choosing *what* to do *when* from a place of wisdom and freedom. Make today the beginning of getting back that control.

PRAYER

Dear God, you have told me that my time is special and precious in so many ways. You have also said that you have made me for specific works. Please help me to see what those are and to make sure that I protect my time and energy to do those things and not a lot of other things that are really not mine to do. Show me my own weaknesses and help me to live a fruitful life. Amen.

eleven

Getting Your Balance Sheet in Order

Freedom is not needing anything from any single person
or entity for survival.

One of the first orders of business or personhood is survival. If a business is dependent upon another entity for survival, then its fate truly is in someone else's hands. There are many nonstrategic situations where a business or a person gets into a relationship that is needed for survival. Whenever that happens, they are at the mercy of however the other person or entity wants to treat them. It could be a business, a boss, a job, a friend or lover, or another relationship. The key indicator is that there is a dependency — financial, emotional, or relational — that is not healthy and keeps someone in bondage.

So what do you do when you realize that you are in a toxic, dependent relationship? If you are truly dependent, you won't survive an abrupt end to the relationship. So you have to recognize the problem and figure out what to do first.

1. Identify a situation in which you have seen someone become so dependent on a person or a client that he or she actually needed that entity in order to survive. What was that situation like, and what were the results?

2. When have you been in that kind of situation, and how much self-control or freedom did you have?

END THE DEPENDENCY

You can never have the freedom of self-control if you are totally dependent on one other person. The reason is that because of what you need from that person, you may not survive the consequences of making the choices you need to make. Freedom, in contrast, is not needing anything from any single person or entity for survival. This does not mean that we do not need people and entities. We do. We survive by needing each other—relationally, emotionally, and financially. The difficulty arises from needing any *one* person or entity in order to survive.

One of the keys to turning around a difficult relationship or to ending a dependent relationship is to have the strength in your corner to be able to do what is necessary to change the situation. If quitting today is not an option, and if staying long term is not an option, the first step is to get your balance sheet in order. Doing so will put you in a position of strength that will enable you to walk away.

3. In what ways do you see how the dependent person in the situation you described in question 1 could have acted differently and had more choices if he or she had been in a position of strength?

4. If you have been in a dependent situation, which choices or behaviors could you have made if you had been operating from a position of strength?

POSITION YOURSELF FOR STRENGTH

If you are going to get in control of your life, you are going to have to do just that—get in control. You have to be able to make the choices that will make your life work, make it belong to you, and integrate it around the things that are important to you. That may require you to set some boundaries and limits with some people. This, of course, is easy to say but hard to do. So you will have to strengthen your personal balance sheet until you are in a position of strength, not a position of dependency.

Moving from a position of dependency to a position of strength requires three things: (1) recognizing the problem, (2) facing the dependency, and (3) building support and strength. Whether the issue is the need to face a difficult boss about mistreatment, to talk to an unreasonable or abusive client, or to confront a spouse who is in denial about an addiction, the strategy for handling the situation is the same. (More scenarios are presented in *The One-Life Solution* book on pages 182–186.)

5. On the chart below, first identify your problem, describe the nature of your dependency, and identify what you can do to build support and strengthen your balance sheet. Identify as many of your dependencies as needed. An example is included to help you get started.

My Problem	My Dependency	My Support for Action
I need to confront a spouse who is in denial about a significant problem, such as substance abuse.	I cannot handle my spouse being upset with me and I know that he or she will be upset if I confront the issue.	I have joined a codependency or support group that is going to stand with me when I confront my spouse's substance problem and will be there for me if things go really badly. I won't be alone.

KEEP BUILDING YOUR EQUITY

Remember, you will not be able to be in control of your own life until you have strengthened your personal balance sheet. Your "equity" must be strong. You need a lot of assets to be who you need to be for yourself and make what you need to have happen, happen; and also to be the servant of others God wants you to be.

6. To increase your equity and build up your balance sheet of life, consider some of the assets you may need from the list below and on the next two pages. As you read through the list, jot down your thoughts about how these equity builders apply to you, as well as specific ways these ideas can help you build the strength you need.

Equity Builders	How I Need to Build My Equity
Develop a strong support system of friends who will stand with you when you have to do something difficult or when you might lose someone's approval or even relationship. Join some existing support groups until your own support system is in place.	
Beef up your skills so that you will have more job opportunities than you want, and more people who need you than you have time for.	
Get more credentials, education, or training not only to raise your marketability but your confidence as well.	

Equity Builders	How I Need to Build My Equity
Focus on business growth so that the vulnerabilities you have to any particular market, customer, or other downturn will not be fatal.	
Get strongly grounded spiritually so that when difficulties occur, relational turmoil happens, or other times of upheaval come, you have a foundation to depend on.	
Find a few people who are specifically dedicated to helping you in the moment of dealing with the crisis (i.e., available to talk to you right before the difficult confrontation, role-play it with you, and be there for you right after and in subsequent weeks).	
Get the coaching, counseling, or mentoring that you need to deal with whatever or whomever you are dealing with in the bigger picture.	

Equity Builders	How I Need to Build My Equity
Get your financial house in order. Get help if you have not been able to accomplish this.	
Develop a dedicated growth path for your relational and life issues.	
Grow in specific relationship and life skills. Take workshops on communication, assertiveness, or conflict resolution so you can face difficult situations with more strength.	
Find a growth community of some sort. That may be a spiritual community, a recovery group, a professional network, or community college, but be a part of a community of people who are getting better at life.	

Remember, the idea here is to build a strong, long-term balance sheet of assets in your life that will enable you to go through whatever circumstances you encounter.

7. How do you think the long-term plan of getting into a position of strength will help you?

8. What will you do to overcome the pull of the urgent problems and remain focused on the long-term fix?

A LAW OF THE UNIVERSE

There is a principle of human functioning that governs your ability to be in control of your life:

Strength and security precede
the ability to be free.

A hungry baby does not walk away from her mother. She does that years later, only after she has had her needs met. A weak, dependent spouse does not walk away from an addict. He does that after he has joined an Al-Anon group to give him the strength. People who have no savings or little chance for another job do not tell an abusive boss to stick it. They do that after they have saved enough money, obtained a degree, or gotten another job. You do not see people who are spiritually and/or relationally bankrupt walk through tough circumstances unscathed. You see them transcend those circumstances as a result of having built spiritual and/or relational equity in their lives.

So, if there is some situation in your life in which you are out of control in a way that is disintegrating your life, heart, soul, or mind, admit to yourself that you have been stuck because you have omitted some personal, spiritual, financial, relational, emotional, or vocational growth in your life that has kept you in a place where you do not want to be. Then, get to work. Identify what deficit is allowing the situation to continue and determine which assets you need to gain first in order to deal with the situation.

You want to stand up but are not strong enough in some way. So here is what I am asking you to do:

Admit that you need to get stronger,
and focus on that first.

YOUR MAIN STRENGTH IS GOD

People, skills, and support systems all play an important role in strengthening our position in life. The Bible talks about these things as specific ways God helps us. For example, Peter tells us that as we give our help to each other, we are "administering God's grace in its various forms" (1 Peter 4:10). So equity-building practices are not only sanctioned by God, but are really a part of how he gives us strength.

As you read these verses, consider what they mean in light of your support systems and skills:

1 Peter 4:10	Each one should use whatever gift he has received to serve others, faithfully administering God's grace in its various forms.
1 Thessalonians 5:14	And we urge you, brothers, warn those who are idle, encourage the timid, help the weak, be patient with everyone.
Hebrews 12:12	Therefore, strengthen your feeble arms and weak knees.
Proverbs 24:5	A wise man has great power, and a man of knowledge increases strength.

9. How does it encourage you to know that to seek help from others (and to give help to others) and to develop your strength, knowledge, and skills is a part of God's plan for you?

God's gifts of people to strengthen us and skills to make us more competent are only a subset of how he makes us stronger. The bigger picture is that God himself is our strength! We must depend on him to not only give us the resources we need, but to give us his strength as we depend on him. Take a look at a few verses about depending on God to be our strength:

Psalm 28:8	The Lord is the strength of his people, a fortress of salvation for his anointed one.
Psalm 29:1	Ascribe to the Lord, O mighty ones, ascribe to the Lord glory and strength.

Psalm 29:11   The LORD gives strength to his people; the LORD blesses his people with peace.

Psalm 46:1   God is our refuge and strength, an ever-present help in trouble.

Psalm 68:35   You are awesome, O God, in your sanctuary; the God of Israel gives power and strength to his people. Praise be to God!

Psalm 84:5   Blessed are those whose strength is in you, who have set their hearts on pilgrimage.

Psalm 84:7   They go from strength to strength, till each appears before God in Zion.

10. Where are you in your own journey of depending on God as your ultimate source of strength and security for life?

11. How do the above verses encourage you to continue building your strength so that you can be set free from the bondage of dependent relationships?

Who will be with you on that journey?

When have you seen God come through for you?

PRAYER

Dear God, I can see that I have been in positions where people or circumstances have controlled me. I confess that to be dependent on any one person allows them to be a god, of sorts, in my life. That is a position that only you should be in, and I desire for you to be the One that I depend on and trust for my security. Help me to see where I am in that position now, and help me to gain the positioning in all of my life to be strong. Lead me to the relationships and alliances that I need to build my foundation to one of strength. Amen

twelve

End Some
Things Now

At times, to make it all work, you will have to end some things.
Some of the things you need to end may be good things.

In life and in work, things end. Relationships end, projects end, careers end, and different seasons of life end. Some endings are planned, and some are forced upon us. Some of them we don't want, yet we find ourselves needing to bring about an end anyway. But one thing is true: If you do not have the ability to end things that need to end, you will never have the one life we have been exploring in this book, and you will always be hampered by problems that should no longer be problems.

1. When have you seen a situation in which the time for an ending has come (or perhaps is long past) but the person involved has resisted that ending to the point that a problem has been allowed to continue without resolution?

What impact has the resistance to an ending had on the person, relationship, or business involved? What has been lost?

NECESSARY ENDINGS

In life, you will get what you tolerate. Period. Problems—and problem people—seek out situations and people who will allow them to exist and to have a space. If you do not tolerate it, they will go away. So, at times, to make it all work, you will have to end some things. While many of those things may be negative, not all of the things you need to end are bad. Now and then you will have to end some good things that are taking up space in your life and keeping you from what is best.

To get to the one life we have been exploring, you are going to have to, for the rest of your life, be committed to two kinds of endings:

- Negative things that are not fixable
- Positive things that are keeping you from the things you care about the most

2. What does the statement, "In life, you will get what you tolerate. Period." say to you about the negative situations you are experiencing in life?

3. What does it take for you to end something negative, and what results have you experienced?

4. When have you had to end something positive in order to make room for something better, and what was the result?

5. Which do you find most difficult to do—end negative things or positive things—and why?

If you are uncomfortable ending things, then you will either delay both of those, or not do them. Either way, you will have predictable results:

- Problems that continue
- Problems that grow into bigger problems
- Mediocrity that you become comfortable with
- Lost opportunity that could have come along by ending something else

While endings are often painful, they are also a necessary part of life. For us to be thriving, and not just surviving, we have to come to grips with that fact of life and get good at executing when the time comes.

6. Why do you think you struggle to end what needs to be ended?

7. Which of the results of resisting endings do you most often see in your life?

How comfortable are you in allowing those resulting conditions to continue?

GET COMFORTABLE WITH ENDINGS

One of the first steps to ending the things we need to end is to get comfortable with the idea of endings. The Bible tells us that endings are a natural part of life: for there to be anything new, like a new tomorrow, old things have to end. To realize that puts us in tune with the way life really is. The idea of endings that make way for what is new is a recurring theme in Ecclesiastes 3:1–8:

> There is a time for everything, and a season for every activity under heaven:
> a time to be born and a time to die, a time to plant and a time to uproot,
> a time to kill and a time to heal, a time to tear down and a time to build,
> a time to weep and a time to laugh, a time to mourn and a time to dance,
> a time to scatter stones and a time to gather them, a time to embrace and a time to refrain,
> a time to search and a time to give up, a time to keep and a time to throw away,
> a time to tear and a time to mend, a time to be silent and a time to speak,
> a time to love and a time to hate, a time for war and a time for peace.

8. In looking at this famous passage from Ecclesiastes, how many endings can you identify in the text?

What are your thoughts about these endings and what they produce?

This passage also conveys the idea of seasons: times for sowing and reaping as well as ending one cycle so the next one can begin. Fall ends one season that leads to planting the next new crop as the new season begins.

Think for a moment about the idea that the concept of "seasons" applies to more than crops — perhaps to jobs, some relationships, involvement in certain activities, and the like.

9. What do you think about the idea that these things can have a "season" too — that it is natural for them to come to an end so that something new can begin?

If it is natural for these to come to an end, is it a mistake to try to keep them going past their life cycle? Why or why not?

10. What is your experience with a life cycle that came to an end and prompted you to move on?

What did that ending lead to that was the "next good thing" for you?

What would you have missed if you had not been able to let go and move on?

11. In what ways are the concepts of positioning yourself for strength (chapter 11) necessary for you as you take steps toward getting good at endings?

There's no getting around the fact that in real life some things must end. In order to move forward toward your goal of having one life, it's time to take an inventory of your relationships and activities to see which ones need to end.

Ending Work Relationships

12. Does someone need to be fired? Why? Why are you resisting?

Do you need to fire a customer? What fears do you need to deal with first?

Ending Activities and Practices

13. Which activities that are taking up time should end and be given to other activities?

What is the good reason these activities existed in the first place, and why might that season be over?

Which toxic or self-destructive practices do you need to end in order to get to where you want to go?

Ending Friendships and Relationships

14. Which friendships or other relationships take up a lot of time but are not the kind of relationships you desire?

What are your fears and resistances toward ending them? What would be the benefit to ending them and moving on?

Which of your significant vital relationships are not getting the time they deserve because other relationships are taking that time? What do you need to end in order to properly balance the relationships?

Which friendships really have little to do with the values or things that are important to you, or worse, actually take you away from the important things? Why are you spending valuable time in those relationships?

15. Which relationships are toxic and hurtful to you? Why do you hold onto them?

16. If you are single, which dating relationships are not taking you where you want to go? Why do you hold onto them?

Ending Financial Practices

17. Which spending practices do you need to end in order to get to where you want to go? (i.e., spending out of desire as opposed to spending according to a budget? spending before giving?)

18. In what ways are you enabling someone financially, and why are you not bringing that to an end?

Remember, some of the things that you want in life are waiting to become realities, but for that to happen, some things have to come to an end.

PRAYER

Dear God, I can see that the nature of life itself is beginnings and endings. As much as I may not like them, endings are a part of life. Please help me to accept this. I know that I have resisted making some of the endings I need to make. Show me which ones those are and the reasons I have resisted. Help me get stronger to be able to do the endings I need to do so that I can live the one life you have designed for me. Amen.

thirteen

Communicating Your Boundaries

In many boundary-setting conversations, the real issue gets lost. Most of us are either too nice, with a tendency to fudge on saying the hard things, or too brutal, forgetting to be caring.

To set limits with people, to define yourself, to say no to people, or to tell people what you want can all be tough things to do. Having those conversations can sometimes cause conflict, separation, guilt, anger, abandonment, rejection, retaliation, and a host of other bad outcomes. You can probably remember at least one time when you told someone something that was necessary and experienced an ugly result. But at the same time, issues must be faced and talked about if things are going to get better. Limits must be set to keep you or someone else from being hurt. Ergo, the conflict: to do what you need to do, you risk relational conflict.

1. To what extent can you identify with the idea that the communication of boundaries and the potential confrontations because of that communication can be difficult for some people?

How difficult are such conversations for you?

2. When have you experienced the bad outcomes of having a difficult conversation with someone?

3. When you are tempted to avoid having a difficult conversation because of fear, what happens inside—your feelings toward the other person, your feelings about yourself, your hope for the relationship—as a result of avoiding the issues you care about?

The wisdom and instruction of the Bible offers some helpful perspectives on our need to communicate what is truly important in the right way, even when it is difficult. Consider, for example:

Leviticus 19:17 Do not hate your brother in your heart. Rebuke your neighbor frankly so you will not share in his guilt.

Ezekiel 3:18 When I say to a wicked man, "You will surely die," and you do not warn him or speak out to dissuade him from his evil ways in order to save his life, that wicked man will die for his sin, and I will hold you accountable for his blood.

4. In what ways do these verses affirm the potential risk of having a difficult conversation?

What is at stake for you and for the other person in such conversations?

What do these verses reveal to you about the importance of such conversations?

Ephesians 4:15 reveals one of the important goals of boundary conversations, and how to approach the conversation: "Instead, speaking the truth in love, we will in all things grow up into him who is the Head, that is, Christ."

5. How does this combination of "truth in love" bring the relationship and the issue together and set the stage for growth?

If it is naturally easy for you to confront people, then your first growth step may be to start to care a little more about how your message is delivered. Often, those who find it too easy to assert themselves —not caring about what the other person feels or thinks—create a wake of broken relationships (personal and professional) that follows them through life. Caring more about others would be a good step to take.

6. If confrontation comes easily to you, have you ever had an experience where you found out that you could have been more sensitive to the person you were confronting? How much of a surprise to you was that experience?

7. Have you ever dealt with or been around someone for whom confrontation came too easily? What feelings did you have about yourself and toward that person as a result of those confrontations?

What have you realized about the importance and impact of difficult conversations as a result of these experiences?

What have you changed in your way of conducting difficult conversations as a result of these experiences?

HOW TO MAKE THE MOST OF A HARD CONVERSATION

In many difficult conversations, such as confrontations and conflicts, the real issues get lost and it is difficult to figure out who actually has the problem because the way the conversation is handled becomes the issue. People go into a conversation to talk about a problem and the conversation is hurtful and the hurt becomes a bigger problem than the original problem was. When an issue is presented in a way that is demeaning, disrespectful, judgmental, or toxic, the outcome is often a new problem to be solved (the hurt that just occurred) and the old problem gets lost in the interaction without ever being resolved.

For a successful outcome, you have to realize that there are two possible ways for a difficult conversation to go badly. First, you may go about it in a way that will make the other person hurt or defensive. Second, you may be dealing with a person who gets hurt and defensive just because the sun comes up every day. The first risk is the only one you can control, but you will be better off by being aware of the second possibility and delivering the news in the best way possible.

8. How much attention have you given to *how* you have difficult conversations so that you can do your best to minimize defensiveness?

What have you found to be helpful and not helpful in presenting your message so that it is actually heard?

The Tone

The way you say things is as important as what you say. People respond to tone as much or more than they do information. If the tone is harsh, demeaning, judgmental, or critical, the person is more likely to fight back, move away, or get defensive. If you are caring and affirming, even when you have to deliver negative information, the other person will be more likely to receive what you are saying. The big tone issues that trigger problematic responses are:

- Anger in your voice
- Aggression in your stance
- Condescending expressions, words, or attitude
- Guilt-inducing words or expressions
- Shame-inducing words, phrases, or implications
- Cold, indifferent demeanor

9. Which of these tone problems has someone ever aimed at you?

What do you remember feeling about your interaction?

How did the tone affect you and your openness to the person?

10. With which of the tone problems listed above have you struggled?

Do you currently have a relationship in which one or more of these is a problem for you? If so, what results of that tone problem are you experiencing?

As is often the case, the Bible clearly expresses the paradox of our human problem and offers advice on how to address it effectively.

James 3:5 identifies our problem with tone: "Likewise the tongue is a small part of the body, but it makes great boasts. Consider what a great forest is set on fire by a small spark." Isn't that exactly what happens? Tone can be so easy to ignore except for the firestorm it sets off!

Ephesians 4:29, 31 shows us a better way to conduct our conversations: "Do not let any unwholesome talk come out of your mouths, but only what is helpful for building others up according to their needs, that it may benefit those who listen. . . . Get rid of all bitterness, rage and anger, brawling and slander, along with every form of malice."

11. What light do these passages shed on what is happening in some of your difficult conversations?

What ideas do they give you on improving your communication and making it more effective?

People can tell when you are for them, and when you are against them or down on them. To begin a conversation with a superior attitude or critical tone is a surefire way to have a negative reaction. So work on softening your tone and avoiding the words that may leave the other person feeling bad. One way to do this is to take a time-out or talk to someone else first to get rid of some of your emotion before you begin what could be a difficult conversation.

Let's consider some additional strategies for helpful boundary conversations.

Affirm the Person, Relationship, and Desired Outcome

Remember, when you come into someone's space with a communication, their brain is scanning to determine whether you are friend or foe. It is asking how to treat the interaction itself. The person's system is either going to be open to the information and to you, or if it perceives a threat, it will go into fight or flight, the natural option for dealing with adversaries. If you begin by letting the person know that you are there as friend, and not foe, and that your desire is to solve a problem so that you can be better friends or work together better, the person is more apt to be open and receptive to you and what you have to say.

12. Think of a potentially difficult conversation that awaits you. What are some ways that you can affirm the person and your relationship in order to set a positive tone for working together toward the desired outcome?

When has someone done this with you, and what was the result?

13. With which people and in which situations do you do a good job of affirmation, and when do you not? Why do you think this is?

Be Specific about the Issue, Not the Person

When talking to a person about an issue, it is vital that you stay away from broad descriptions and labeling of the person's character. Our common attempts at getting someone to perform better often sound something like this: "You're so irresponsible. I want you to be more responsible in your work habits and act as if you care."

This approach is primed for failure. It makes the person feel crummy, and it doesn't give them anything specific to work on. A better approach is to drop the negative labels, state the specific problem, and give clear expectations of what you want to have happen.

14. How do you feel when someone describes your character with broad, negative labels instead of telling you what they want you to do?

15. Think back to a time when you were broad and negative in handling a difficult conversation, and rewrite a better, more specific way you could have approached the issue.

Do the same thing for a difficult conversation you *anticipate* having.

Get Agreement

In problematic interactions in which there is the possibility for defensiveness, denial, or oversensitivity, it is important to get agreement after the conversation to ensure that both of you are on the same page. So check it out at the end. If the person has heard you say something that you are not saying, then clarify it with them then and there until you both understand the real message that you are intending to convey.

16. In which situations would it have been better for you to check it out at the end, and what happened as a result of not doing that?

For which of your *current* situations and relationships would it be good to practice "getting agreement" on what was said?

In addition to getting agreement about what you have said, get agreement about what is going to happen in the future. Define the behaviors you need from the person in order to accomplish the goal you desire. Make sure that you both understand what you are expecting and that there is agreement to fulfill that expectation.

17. In which current relationships would you do well to get clear agreement on what the expectations are for the future?

Balance Care and the Whole Truth

We began this chapter by seeing that most of us, stylistically, are either too nice with a tendency to fudge on saying the hard things, or too brutal, forgetting to be caring. The effective communicator, however, shows care for the person and does not skirt the issue at all. If you can do both, then you will get the best results, even from the most difficult people.

A good guiding principle is to "go hard on the issue and soft on the person." Hard on the issue means that you are not going to fudge on saying what you need to say about the problem at hand. Soft on the person means that you are going to be caring and compassionate while you are steadfast in your position. You are going to be immovable and steadfast, but not aggressive, domineering, or hostile. The Bible's words for this are "grace and truth."

18. Can you think of an example where "hard on the issue" and "hard on the person" has been done to you? How did you feel, and what was the outcome?

Can you think of an example of "soft on the issue" and "soft on the person" that has been done to you? How did you feel, and what was the outcome?

In either of these examples, how would "hard on the issue and soft on the person" have made a difference?

In which situation right now do you need to repair being too soft on the issue, or too hard on the person?

Hold On to Your Perspective through Separateness

When you are going to communicate, remember to remain separate from the other person. This means that you make sure that his issue, perspective, defensiveness, feelings, or opinions do not become your own unless you choose to make them yours. You need to be aware of this because your personal power drains can cause you to lose your sense of separateness. Then the other person's agenda becomes yours and your agenda is abandoned.

19. Can you identify with having lost your sense of separateness when communicating with someone who was strong or defensive? What happened to your agenda in the process?

If there is a person with whom you tend to lose your separateness, what power drain do you think is causing your lack of control?

In your communication with a person who tries to bring you over to his or her side, emphasize your separateness by clearly stating so as often as needed. Some people need frequent reminders of your separateness, and those reminders will help you keep your position too. So make it clear for them. "I understand that you think A. But my perspective is different than that. I think B."

20. What are your best strategies to stay separate in your communications with the person(s) with whom you tend to lose it?

Which specific phrases can you use to keep your agenda intact? Practice saying them!

Stay Separate from the Difficult Person

The idea of staying separate when people are defensive or in denial is very important. Their strategy is to not have to take ownership of whatever it is that you are trying to get them to own. So they will deflect, excuse, minimize, blame, or throw out a whole host of responses to keep from being responsible. When they do, staying separate from all of that noise is important. Staying separate from all of their attempts to avoid responsibility means that you will not get sidetracked and lose the focus of what you are trying to communicate.

21. If you can identify with having confronted someone only to receive defensive or attacking behavior as a result, what was that like for you and what was the result?

To what extent did you "lose yourself," or your separate message in the process?

To remain separate from people in difficult conversations, you must stay in touch with what you want and what you think. Do not get talked out of your agenda unless you are truly being shown the light. The formula for remaining separate is to empathize and return to the issue. Do not take the bait and let go of yourself. Instead, empathize and return to your issue.

22. In which relationships or situations do you need to practice this formula?

What statements can you use to empathize with those specific people?

What statements can you use to direct those specific people back to your issue, your side of the conversation?

Set Limits

Limits are basically the boundary line that says how far you are going to go with a certain issue. It could be a behavior, an attitude, or a time issue. It may be a financial limit, or how much you will agree to do for someone before you begin to feel as if you are being used. It may be to limit the degree of freedom that someone has with you to not live up to certain commitments. Whatever the context, a limit says how far you will allow something to go, and how far you won't. When it comes to limits, you get what you tolerate.

23. In which experiences would you have saved some pain or trouble had you set limits?

Why do you think you didn't set limits and what were the results?

If you had it to do over again, what limits would you set and how?

The first step in setting limits is to simply confront the behavior, using all of the appropriate principles we have already explored. Affirm the relationship or the person, along with the outcome, and get your tone in order. Be specific, and talk about what you want to focus on and what you want to see that is different. If the person listens, then all is well. The limit has contained the destructive behavior and not allowed it to spread.

24. Think of a behavior that you currently need to confront. What would your limit-setting statement be?

    Does your statement affirm? Is it specific about the problem? Does it clearly identify the desired outcome?

    What do you feel when you anticipate delivering this statement? Fear? Confidence? Why?

Sometimes, a simple limit is not enough. More is needed. A boundary without consequences is only a suggestion. Real boundaries have real teeth to back them up. At some point it is time to invoke consequences, time to deliver the "don't think I won't do that" talk.

25. How do you feel about having to initiate a "don't think I won't do that" talk? Does it feel mean to you, or are you afraid to do it?

    How do your feelings change when you realize that talking without consequences has not helped and that further talking without consequences is not going to help either?

Communicating Your Boundaries   163

26. In which situation right now do you need to have the "don't think I won't do that" talk or actually begin to set consequences into action?

If you know you need to but are not setting consequences, why are you not doing it? What are your fears and expectations of taking this step or of not taking it?

TIPS TO HELP YOU CARRY THROUGH

Having difficult conversations about problems is almost never easy, but as we have seen, it is very important. Now that you know the big-picture principles and process of handling boundary conversations, consider applying the following tips that can help you conduct that difficult conversation successfully.

Strength in Numbers: Bring Others with You

Other people can give you strength and help create a stronger boundary for the person with the problem. Other people also serve as witnesses if further action is needed. Matthew 18:15 – 18 shows how this practice works:

> If your brother sins against you, go and show him his fault, just between the two of you. If he listens to you, you have won your brother over. But if he will not listen, take one or two others along, so that "every matter may be established by the testimony of two or three witnesses." If he refuses to listen to them, tell it to the church; and if he refuses to listen even to the church, treat him as you would a pagan or a tax collector. I tell you the truth, whatever you bind on earth will be bound in heaven, and whatever you loose on earth will be loosed in heaven.

27. When have you seen the power of more than one person not only bring courage to confront someone who is difficult, but also "bind" or contain the problem person as well?

What have you learned from that situation that you would do well to apply to a current difficult situation you face?

Plan the Conversation about the Conversation

Sometimes, as we have seen, talking about the problem does not help. It is then time to talk about how talking is not helping. This conversation shows the person that there is a bigger problem than the issue at hand: that it does no good to try to address problems with the person. This conversation makes it clear that the bigger problem can be a deal breaker. The frank reality of this approach often breaks through the person's denial.

28. Are you in a situation where you have talked and talked about the problem and nothing is helping? When will you take the step to talk about the fact that talking is not helping and that the bigger problem must be addressed?

Make a Plan

When talking has not helped, and you fear that the problem could happen again, you may want to have a conversation about making a plan. It is an "I know you have said that you will not do it again, and that is great. But let's get agreement as to what we will do if that occurs, so we both know what will happen then."

29. With whom do you need to agree on a plan for future action?

Role-Play

Difficult people can render you less able to think in a heated or defensive conversation. That is why it can be important to practice. Practice helps you know what you want to say, gives you courage to say it, and helps you stay on track when you need to do it.

30. In which situations have you become flustered and lost the ability to say what you needed to say?

What would it have been worth to you to have completed that conversation successfully? Would a little practice have been worth the result?

Who can help you role-play a difficult conversation for next time?

PEOPLE ARE NOT THE SAME

When dealing with people, one size does not fit all. The Bible, as well as experience, tells us that people are not the same. You can talk to some people and get good results. They listen and correct their behavior. For these people, the observation of Proverbs 9:8 is true: "Rebuke a wise man and he will love you."

31. With whom in your life have you been able to give feedback and see that it leads to good things in the relationship?

Other people, however, are more difficult. You can talk, but they do not easily listen. They do not take initial feedback well and often do not follow through with changes. The Bible offers advice for dealing with these people as well: "Do not rebuke a mocker or he will hate you" (Proverbs 9:8), and "Do not speak to a fool, for he will scorn the wisdom of your words" (Proverbs 23:9). With these people you must stop talking about the problem and move to the consequences.

32. Who in your life falls into this category, and have you decided it is time to stop talking and start the consequences? If not, why not?

What results do you expect as a result of your action or inaction?

The third category of people are the ones where even consequences do not help. With these people, there is usually no hope and you just have to protect yourself, others, or your organization. Ending the relationship or exercising legal protection is necessary. The Bible gives advice for dealing with these people as well—"A prudent man sees danger and takes refuge, but the simple keep going and suffer for it" (Proverbs 22:3)—which shows the importance of recognizing real danger and getting away to protect yourself or others.

33. Is there someone in your situation now with whom talking, consequences, or other interventions have not helped and you must protect yourself?

What protective measures are you taking?

If you are not protecting yourself, what is keeping you from doing so?

Remember, you will get what you tolerate, and communicating your boundaries is the way that you show where the line actually is of what you will tolerate and what you will not. Do whatever you need to do to become someone who has the skills and the courage to speak the words that are needed to "bind on earth" what needs to be bound. And know that God is with you.

PRAYER

Dear God, I thank you that you have shown us that we are your mouthpieces to speak truth into sometimes difficult situations. I thank you also that you have shown us how to do that with love and grace. Sometimes, I confess, it is difficult for me to do; I fear the consequences and do not do the hard things that are necessary. Help me to see where I need to take the next step, and help me to have the courage and the skills and to find the help and support I need to do that. Amen.

From This Day Forward

Congratulations on finishing your journey through this workbook. I am sure that the soul-searching, and the sharing and support you experienced if you did this in a group, were worth the time spent. As we've already discussed, this kind of activity is "vital." So, way to go in spending your time and energy, your greatest resources, in a wise manner.

As with all kinds of growth, the real payoff is in the follow-up, the follow-through, and the implementation of the changes you have decided are important. So, I wanted to end the workbook with a word of encouragement for you to not see this as an ending, but as a beginning. But, as I thought about it, it can actually be both.

My prayer for you is that this is an end not only to the automatic patterns that have dominated your time and energy for so long, but also to having other people or situations be in control of your life. Let's agree to end those patterns right now, no matter where they came from or what sustained them. It is time for you to reclaim your life so that you can be the steward God intends you to be and accomplish your vision and his call for your life.

And, in addition to an end to old patterns that have robbed you and the ones you care about, now can also be a beginning of a whole new way of living, the way that God designed you to live: a life marked by self-control. When you are in control of your life, you are free to follow not only God's purposes for you, but also the dreams of your heart. But to do that, this has to be a beginning of putting into practice the things you learned in this book about your life and about yourself. It means remaining in the process of growth itself, not seeing this as a "one-time event," but as a new way of living.

I would encourage you to continue down the path of self-examination before God and a few people who care about you and will help you. If you put into practice the things God shows you, you will be amazed at the difference in your life, at its fruitfulness, and your fulfillment.

About the Author

Dr. Henry Cloud (www.drcloud.com) is a clinical psychologist with extensive experience in private practice, leadership consulting, business, and media. Drawing from over twenty years of experience in many contexts, he simplifies life's issues and gives easy-to-understand, practical advice to both business leaders and mass audiences. He is the author of several bestselling books, including *Boundaries, Integrity,* and *9 Things You Simply Must Do,* and he has been featured or reviewed in many publications, including the *New York Times,* the *Los Angeles Times,* and the *Boston Globe.* Dr. Cloud has been a guest on numerous radio and television shows.

Dr. Cloud's leadership consulting focuses on CEO and executive coaching, team building, and board and management relations. He speaks frequently at large public conferences and in corporate settings, on both leadership and personal growth topics.

To inquire about leadership coaching, executive development, or consulting, or to book Dr. Cloud for a speaking engagement, send requests to:

bookings@drcloud.com

The One-Life Solution

The Boundaries Way to Integrating Work and Life

Henry Cloud

Dr. Henry Cloud, author of the bestselling Boundaries series, is a clinical psychologist known for his remarkable ability to clarify life's most complex dilemmas. Now, in *The One-Life Solution*, he turns his attention to what for many Americans is one of the most difficult problems they face: in an era of ceaseless communication, when jobs don't stop when you leave the office, and ever-increasing complexity, how can readers integrate life and work so as to achieve happiness and success at both?

With the straightforward tools Dr. Cloud provides, even the most harried professional torn between demanding bosses, coworkers, clients, and the pressures of family and personal life will be able to implement *The One-Life Solution* to find success and happiness.

Hardcover, Jacketed: 978-0-06-146642-7

Pick up a copy today at your favorite bookstore!

Boundaries in Marriage

Dr. Henry Cloud and Dr. John Townsend

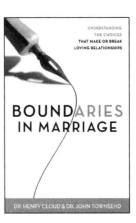

Learn when to say yes and when to say no — to your spouse and to others — to make the most of your marriage.

Only when a husband and wife know and respect each other's needs, choices, and freedom can they give themselves freely and lovingly to one another. Boundaries are the "property lines" that define and protect husbands and wives as individuals. Once they are in place, a good marriage can become better, and a less-than-satisfying one can even be saved.

Drs. Henry Cloud and John Townsend, counselors and authors of the award-winning bestseller *Boundaries*, show couples how to apply the ten laws of boundaries that can make a real difference in relationships. They help husbands and wives understand the friction points or serious hurts and betrayals in their marriage — and move beyond them to the mutual care, respect, affirmation, and intimacy they both long for.

Boundaries in Marriage helps couples:

- Set and maintain personal boundaries and respect those of their spouse
- Establish values that form a godly structure and architecture for their marriage
- Protect their marriage from different kinds of "intruders"
- Work with a spouse who understands and values boundaries — or work with one who doesn't

Softcover: 978-0-310-24314-4

Pick up a copy today at your favorite bookstore!

Boundaries with Kids

How Healthy Choices Grow Healthy Children

Dr. Henry Cloud and Dr. John Townsend

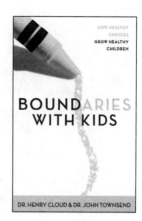

What the award-winning *Boundaries* has done for adult relationships, *Boundaries with Kids* will do for you and your children.

Here is the help you need for raising your kids to take responsibility for their actions, attitudes, and emotions. Drs. Henry Cloud and John Townsend take you through the ins and outs of instilling the kind of character in your children that will help them lead balanced, productive, and fulfilling adult lives.

Learn how to

- set limits and still be a loving parent
- bring control to an out-of-control family life
- apply the ten laws of boundaries to parenting
- define appropriate boundaries and consequences for your kids

    ... and much more.

"Boundaries with Kids helps us give our kids the skills they need to live realistic and full lives in meaningful relationships. Not perfect—but healthy!"

—Elisa Morgan, president of MOPS International, Inc.

Softcover: 978-0-310-24315-1

Pick up a copy today at your favorite bookstore!

Share Your Thoughts

With the Author: Your comments will be forwarded to the author when you send them to *zauthor@zondervan.com*.

With Zondervan: Submit your review of this book by writing to *zreview@zondervan.com*.

Free Online Resources at
www.zondervan.com

Zondervan AuthorTracker: Be notified whenever your favorite authors publish new books, go on tour, or post an update about what's happening in their lives.

Daily Bible Verses and Devotions: Enrich your life with daily Bible verses or devotions that help you start every morning focused on God.

Free Email Publications: Sign up for newsletters on fiction, Christian living, church ministry, parenting, and more.

Zondervan Bible Search: Find and compare Bible passages in a variety of translations at www.zondervanbiblesearch.com.

Other Benefits: Register yourself to receive online benefits like coupons and special offers, or to participate in research.